Who's Afear'd

First published in 2005 by Parnham Press, Beaminster, Dorset
© 2005 Parnham Press, UK

ISBN 0-9550712-0-8
A catalogue record for this book is available from the British Library

Text © 2005 Michael Feasey
All photographs © 2005 Brian Neesam
Edited by Antonia Johnson
Designed by Mike Bone, Bostock and Pollitt Ltd, London

2005 / 10 9 8 7 6 5 4 3 2 1
Printed in the UK by Remous Ltd, Sherborne, Dorset

Printed on Consort Renew-Satin, supplied by Howard Smith Paper,
Consort Renew-Satin is manufactured from TCF pulp and produced
through a totally acid-free process. All grammages are 50% recycled
and the pulp is sourced from sustainable managed forests

parnham press

Eat Dorset

By Michael Feasey with
photographs by Brian Neesam

Parnham Press

Contents

Foreword

EAT DORSET WAS conceived about two and a half years ago after I and my husband Michael had moved to Dorset from London. The restoration of the house was complete, I was living full time in Dorset with all four of my children at local day schools, so I began to turn my attention to a new project.

I had no previous experience of publishing and I very seldom ever cook, and so when I announced to my husband that I wanted to publish a cook book he nearly fell off his chair laughing. I frequently met friends at dinner parties who would reveal in hushed tones their sources for delicious smoked fish, the best bread and fabulous cheeses. There seemed to be an abundance of choice, but often actually finding the foods was not so easy – you needed to be in the know. Luckily at about that time I met Mike Feasey the food writer, and we set to work devising a book that described the landscape, the people and the produce, through photographs and words. I felt that the quality of the local food could really only be understood within the context of the surroundings.

A fundamental element of *Eat Dorset's raison d'être* is fundraising for charity. I was looking for something that was longer lasting than an event, and where I could enjoy the process as well as raising proceeds for good causes. My primary interest is in the care of children, and the three charities that benefit from this book are all concerned with the well-being of children and families. I have supported the NSPCC in its fight against child abuse for many years, and lately I have been working with two local charities, the Beaminster Playgroup, who have no government funding and are in dire need of new premises, and the Dorset Child and Family Counselling Trust, who provide therapy to disrupted families.

Publishing a book was a bit of a challenge although very rewarding. The real story behind the book however is the amazing generosity of everyone involved, who gave their time and talents selflessly, and it is thanks to them that *Eat Dorset* came to being.

There is another aspect to this book: the relationship between mankind and the environment. Suffice it to say that I hope the book will inspire you to buy local produce, in season, and maybe spend a little more on food; to consider how far it has travelled, and what good in the long term it will do for you or the environment – or what harm. Consider also the interests of animals and the methods used to keep prices low. One last thought, as we are entering a new phase of the EU and a re-assessment of the Common Agricultural Policy seems inevitable: only by more active participation from the consumer can the various farming and food producing activities touched on in the book thrive. They set a new standard in alternative, but increasingly mainstream, forward-thinking practices. I hope others will follow. In some ways it would seem we have come full cycle and the future is somewhere buried in the past.

Emma Treichl

Acknowledgements
There are a great many people to whom I owe an enormous amount of thanks. Mike Feasey and Brian Neesam, the writer and the photographer, who have given their time and talents for free. The committee (Helen Carless, Sophie Digby, Rose Joly, Tilly McMaster, Juli Neesam, Diana Pinney, Tessa Russell and Annette Smallwood) have been fantastic; Antonia Johnson in particular for all her hard work editing and proof-reading the book; Mike Bone from Bostock and Pollitt, who has done all the layouts and designed the look of the book, also entirely gratis; Mark Ashley-Miller, who generously gave us access to the Present Finder website (www.thepresentfinder.co.uk), enabling us to sell directly to the public and thereby generate even more for the charities involved; Valentine Villiers who navigated us through the publishing world; and Portfolio Press who had the confidence to distribute us nationwide. Thanks also go to Howard Smith Paper who supplied paper at cost. Thank you all.

Introduction

A GREAT PART of my youth was spent on the south coast of Dorset. I have fond memories of Blue Vinney cheese, Eldridge Pope ales, and night-fishing for tasty sea bass. Most of my adult life in England was spent living and working in London, and I moved back to West Dorset with my partner Claire in 2002, after spending some fine weekends camping in Lulworth with friend Brian Neesam (*Eat Dorset's* photographer) and his family. Most of the foods I remembered as very worthy were still good, but I was surprised to come across a chilli farm (see page 39) – Dorset was more exotic than I expected. I did some detective work and soon realised I was only scratching the surface of a centre of food excellence.

Dorset's diversity of lush produce reflects its soil and climate, although in recent history food was not plentiful for everyone. In the early 19th century, farm workers had little to live on – this is the county where social unrest led to the persecution of the Tolpuddle Martyrs. Agriculture and fishing were the main industries, and Portland and its quarries also played a part in the local economy, but many of the working class folk supplemented their diet from the wild. Rooks and rabbits, sorrel and wild lettuce; hedgerows provided blackberries, crab-apples and sloes, on the beach shellfish, sea kale and samphire could be harvested.

The key element that bound the population, regardless of class or background, was the knowledge of when food was available. I have followed this natural calendar in *Eat Dorset*, showing the reader what to expect to find by scheduling recipes according to the seasons. My photographer friend, Brian Neesam, has captured timely images over the course of the year.

My publisher liked the informal style of my food column in *Dorset* magazine, so it follows that the recipes are set out in user-friendly terms without cheffy jargon, intending to inspire the user rather than test him or her with difficult methods or hard-to-source ingredients. I have attempted to show our county's produce in the best light and cooking styles and spicing are often global in influence – something I make no apology for. Not that there isn't nobility in classic country foods, but there are many other books that have this subject area well-covered. With *Eat Dorset* I have attempted to move the goalposts a little further on.

The following recipe that illustrates a traditional food source is supplied by Jeremy 'Jamie' Pope, west Dorset resident and a neighbour. He has a life-long interest in food and wine and is a keen shot, gardener and cook, inflicting the various fruits of these activities on family and friends.

ROOK PIE

Cut steak into bite-sized strips, chop mushrooms and blanch shallots in boiling water for a few minutes, drain, then glaze with Madeira (reduced by bubbling in a saucepan until syrupy).

Roll out pastry (8mm thick) to cover a deep pie dish, with an extra strip to provide a seal around the dish. Place a support in the centre of the pie dish, and put in ingredients – beef, rook, mushroom and shallots – in layers, season, and pour warmed stock over. Cut a cross of about 2.5cm in centre of the pie crust and crimp this up, so that it fits over the support. Dampen the pie dish support and seal with water before placing the crust over the pie, attaching the cross to the support and crimping the crust around the rim of the dish with a fork to form a seal. Brush the cover with beaten egg and decorate.

Bake in hot oven (200°C/gas mark 6) until crust is golden (about 15-20 mins) then turn down to 140°C/gas mark 3/4 for about 1 hour to cook meat. Remove, lift off crust carefully and add cream to cover meat. Allow to cool and serve cold.

Serves: 4-6 (starter)
Preparation time: 35 minutes
Cooking time: 1½ hours

240g good aged rump steak, fat/sinews removed

breasts of 8 young rooks

120g mushrooms

120g shallots, small, peeled, whole

good dash of Madeira, well reduced

360g pastry (240g plain flour, 120g butter, 2 tbsp water)

Strong veal/jelly stock (page 60)

275ml thick double cream

Maldon sea salt and freshly ground black pepper

1 medium egg, beaten, for eggwash

Spring

A vast journey

SUNNYSIDE FARM IS a working organic farm at Lower Kingcombe, farmed by the very able Mandie Fletcher and her partner Sweetpea. The farm and the surrounding 600 acres of Dorset Wildlife Trust land are Sites of Special Scientific Interest because of their ancient hay meadows and historic pasture, and the farm is obliged to follow time-consuming programmes to preserve this exceptional part of the English countryside (laying hedges, for instance). They also have a beautifully converted cow byre for rent, 'The Old Barn', which sleeps 2-6, from which you can explore the landscape.

Mandie entered the farming world via an unexpected background: she has a distinguished career in television comedy and you'll notice her directing credits on some hugely popular shows – *Blackadder* and *Only Fools and Horses* amongst many. With such firm credentials under her televisual belt she is able to pick and choose her projects at will, and this frees her up to concentrate on her other love, farming. She confessed that it was purely by chance she ended up at Sunnyside. She had been searching for a home for her horse, and fell in love with the farm. It was, she says, 'so attractive to me, that it was simply a case of not wanting anyone else to bugger it up'. So it became her home, too. She sought the advice of the retiring farmer, who had already achieved Soil Association organic certification for the land, and he acted as mentor and guide on all matters agricultural. This was, as you would expect, not something to be absorbed in a season. The land was somewhat overgrazed at the beginning and Mandie reduced the stocking levels, the meat continuing to be organically reared and homeopathically treated if necessary. The animals are grass-reared and wintered outside; one of the benefits according to Mandie being very tender flesh. The animals are bought in from The Dorset Wildlife Trust – as Mandie says, laughing – it is too stressful to have to get up and deal with calving problems in the middle of the night. A stress-free environment is important for animals too, particularly at the time of slaughter. When the stock is ready, it is carefully tended, being led singly onto transport with a steadying hand, and taken to Snell's in Chard.

Sweetpea and Mandie work hard to produce organic beef and lamb, and a succulent variety of seasonal vegetables and salad from their market garden. Mandie enjoys being part of a successful organic community and is thrilled to introduce new people to good food. Sweetpea is part of the creativity that has supported the 'Eat less meat and better quality' philosophy that Mandie is absolutely hooked on. They market their own tomato-based pasta sauces and thyme-enhanced beefburgers, popular with visitors staying at the barn. Sweetpea is proud to recount some escapees from London relishing some chard she cooked for them so much, she was told she actually 'changed the visitors' eating habits for life'. Certainly something to be proud of.

Chard can change your life

Sweetpea and Mandie realise they are extremely lucky to be neighbours of the Kingcombe Centre just a few yards' stroll up the lane, who they also supply with meat.

Mandie is seeing all her hard work of the last 6 years come to fruition. It has been, as she tells me, a vast journey, considering she was only looking to graze her horse! Here is a winning curry recipe that always wows her visitors.

MUTTON AND CHARD CURRY

Brown the mutton in batches in the oil and set aside. Add butter (or ghee), onion, garlic and soften. Add the paste and fry off a couple of minutes. Add coconut milk and stock or water. Return browned mutton to the pot, add lentils and cook slowly in a low oven (160°C/ gas mark 3) for 2–2½ hours.

Finally, shred chard into very thin ribbons and sink into the cooked curry for 5 minutes or until soft. Serve with rice.

Serves: 4
Preparation time: 20 minutes
Cooking time: 2½ hours

400g diced organic mutton

1 tbsp vegetable oil

25g ghee (or butter)

1 heaped tbsp Patak's cumin & chilli paste

1 onion, medium chopped

3 cloves garlic, peeled, sliced

150g red lentils

1 x 415g tin coconut milk

100ml water or stock

200g washed chard

salt to taste

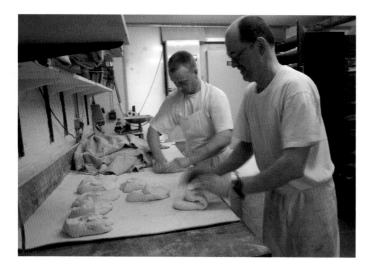

Sourdough traditions

LONG CRICHEL IS a small village in the eastern quadrant of Dorset noteworthy for its artisan bakery. Owners Jamie and Rose Campbell lead the team, with able help from Kay Tanner, master baker Scott, and Katherine to manage the marketing. The bakery's huge wood-fired oven was designed by Jamie with the help of consultant Paul Merry, head tutor at the Panary bakery school. It features a natural brick floor construction with side-vents that draw the heat from the ash-wood fires at the side of the oven, across the main oven area through to the back wall. Batches of dough are baked on one level, at one temperature, that slowly declines as the ferocity of the flames die back, although greater constancy can be achieved by feeding more wood into the furnace. The oven's source of heat is big enough for two bakings and can handle a maximum of 70kg of dough at optimum temperature – about 350°C, once the flames are out. White breads go in first, at the back, using a large long-handled wooden paddle to shuffle the breads around to get maximum use of the space, and then the other flour types, all arranged according to the sensitivity of the product, with the ryes and buns going in last.

Their range of breads is magnificent, with pride of place being given to their excellent sourdoughs. This type of breadmaking uses long-fermented sourdough mixes according to old European traditional methods, and is nothing like the mass-production Chorleywood methods used by industrial-size conglomerates. Some of the naturally-derived yeasts that initiate the sourdoughs are derived from airborne cultures that give grapes their bloom. Jamie is rightly proud of his sourdough range and considers he led the way for some while; he even puts a little sourdough 'mother' mix into his croissants. Imported Eastern European grains like spelt are more and more popular with customers, although most of the flour comes from English crops milled by Stoate's and Shipton Mills.

Alongside Long Crichel breads you will find mouth-watering savouries, croissants, buns and sweet pastries. You must try their Benedict Bars – a very rich almond and luscious raspberry confection on a shortbread base that is the nearest and best thing to a true Bakewell pudding I've come across.

Over the road a high brick wall hides a patch of land owned by Jamie and Rose, where Anni Sax runs Long Crichel Organics. There is a symbiotic relationship with the bakery, who use the seasonal vegetable and fruit in their recipes. The garden of just over 2 acres is Soil Association certified, and there are 150 trees that bear either fruit or nuts. It is too small to make her a living, so Anni has a number of allied projects on the go, including arranging tours and lessons in gardening for children and adults with learning difficulties, working with local authorities – as she maintains, it really pays to educate people about nature.

Seasonal fruit and veg gets boxed up at Long Crichel Organics

Liquid assets

DORSET'S MANOR FARM has been farmed for the last 71 years by
the Best family, and the award-winning business is currently run by the
charming Will and Pam Best. Situated in the South Wessex Downs
at Godmanstone, the dedicated duo practice a mixed-farming policy,
keeping about 80 cows, plus sheep, as well as growing a variety of arable
crops. They have been at the forefront of the environmentally-sensitive
but demanding Soil Association movement, with full organic status
on all land and stock since 1988. The Bests' cows enjoy homeopathic
treatments courtesy of Phil the herdsman.

Like all good farmers, Will and Pam believe that food should be
processed as little as possible, so they draw the line at homogenising their
milk, and never will. Great news for people like me who rate the top-of-
the-milk as just perfect over their cornflakes. Will's vision has always been
clear. Milk is after all an important staple food for most people, especially
children, and it should be as pure and unadulterated as possible and, of
course, taste good. He believes he's got the best milk (and cream) around.

Now whip yourself up a cream frenzy with this luscious recipe.

CANDIED GINGER AND RUM CRÈME BRULÉE

Place cream and pods in a saucepan, heat to just below boiling point.
Set aside to cool (5 minutes). Preheat oven (160°–180°C/gas mark 3-4).
Remove pods, scraping remaining vanilla paste back into mix. Discard pods.

Whisk yolks with sugar until creamy, stir in warm cream and rum.
Grease eight ramekins and fill to 1cm from top. Place foil squares over
pots, smooth down sides to form level covers. Use a *bain-marie* with
boiling water (level halfway up sides). Bake for 15-17 minutes. If too
wobbly, bake for another few minutes. Cool and refrigerate.

Uncover, place 4-5 slices of ginger on top and sprinkle a sugar layer
3-5mm over entire surface. Preheat grill (maximum), placing pots close
to grill, melt sugar to caramel. When golden to dark brown, remove and
allow to cool. Serve slightly chilled.

Serves: 8
Preparation time: 20 minutes
Cooking and cooling time:
2½ hours

3 vanilla pods, split

8 egg yolks

2 tbsp caster sugar

600ml Manor Farm
double cream

2 tbsp dark rum
(Appletons Gold is good)

Unsalted butter for greasing

3 stem gingers, thinly sliced
into 2mm discs

Demerara sugar (not Muscovado)
to caramelise

Native culture

IN THE NOVEL Moonfleet, J. Meade-Falkner mentions the Fleet lagoon as 'good for nothing except sea-fowl, herons and oysters'. Today, it is a nature reserve, a natural estuary that runs from the Ferry Bridge end of the Isle of Portland (strictly speaking, a peninsula), as far up as the village of Abbotsbury, where the Swannery is. The Fleet Oyster Farm raises oysters on the lagoon. The current owner Nigel Bloxham changed the name from Abbotsbury Oysters as visitors were travelling mistakenly to Abbotsbury some 7 miles away.

The lagoon is enchanting, with clean, mineral and plankton-rich waters, essential elements for oysters, real grade-A water for 11 months of the year. Unfortunately for Nigel's consultant Peter Hoare, due to the swans upstream nesting and breeding in May and June the water is messed up, resulting in the lesser 'B' grade. But Peter seems to take this problem in his stride. To meet the EU's hygiene regulations they need to purify shellfish under UV-illuminated filtration for about 48 hours, and keep them in aerated holding tanks until sold. This they do all year round, to maintain public confidence in the quality of the oysters even though they are grown in such pure waters.

Although they do farm a few natives, the bulk of the annual harvest are Pacifics. Graded and sold by weight – 80g, 90g, 100g and 110g – they are markedly salty, and less gamy than the natives, with plenty of meat and a firm texture. As they are so meaty, they are also very good for cooking. The season starts in April and Peter is adamant that good oysters should not be available until then. He claims to know his onions as far as recipes are concerned: natives should be enjoyed straight from the shell with some lemon and pepper, but he also loves oysters Kilpatrick with *lardons* of bacon and some Lea & Perrins, and he recommends Russian oysters, using Pacifics, whose deep shells are perfect for adding toppings.

Customers of Fleet Oysters can either opt for take-away, or sit by the lagoon in The Crab House Café and be served ready-opened oysters with French bread and a glass of wine or a good cold lager. Other local seafood delights are also available.

Peter's Russian oysters sound pretty good, so here's how.

Serves: 4
Preparation time: 20 minutes

16 large oysters, opened, chilled

100ml thick double cream

60g quality caviar

1 tbsp (about 25ml) premium-grade iced vodka (Peter recommends a rubber-tipped pipette for 'dosing' oysters) giving 3-4 drops per serving

RUSSIAN OYSTERS
Open oysters carefully and ensure juice is kept in the shell, add a dollop of thick double cream, a teaspoonful of good caviar and a few drops of premium vodka – eat!

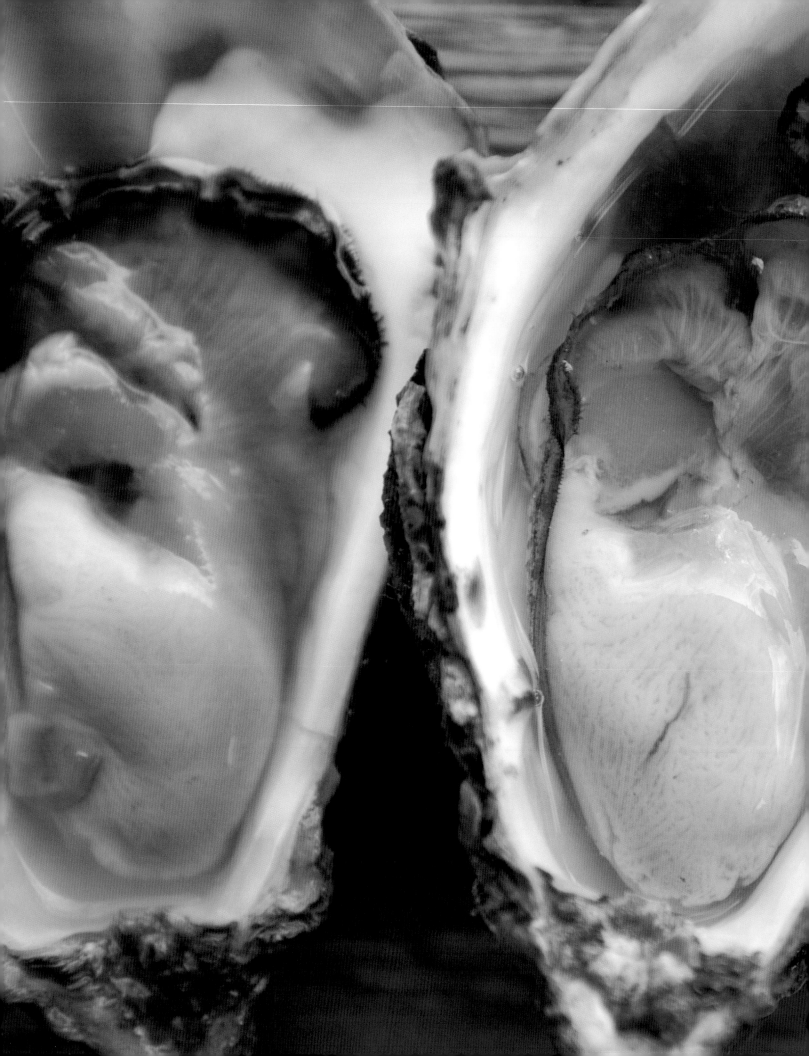

Growing tips

THERE'S SOMETHING OF a supply problem, if you want to buy locally-grown asparagus on a commercial scale. Research names famous growers in neighbouring Hampshire, also Kent, Lincolnshire and East Anglia... but here? Zilch! I asked around and eventually discovered Vicky Kardas, a grower based at Coldharbour near Wareham. She has a mixed business, Oakland's Plantation, selling via her own farm shop and through Dorchester, Wimborne and Swanage markets, featuring blueberries, raspberries, various mixed orchard fruits and even, recently, ornamentals.

But it's the green stuff I'm interested in. So how come it's hard to find local commercially-grown asparagus? It's partly because of the soil type: ideally it needs rich, well-drained, sandy soil without acidity – which would not be ideal for their other main crop, blueberries. So Vicky had to find a slope that although mostly clay-based, would allow a suitable harvest because of the drainage. They ploughed trenches with newspaper at the bottom, initially to protect the delicate crowns – to keep them warm at the critical early period – then put in well-matured horse manure and lime, well-covered with good soil; it's easy to 'scorch' the roots if you're not careful. If you get two-year old crowns to start you off rather than seed you're able to harvest the following year. I asked whether it was that easy – simply bung in the plant, wait for tips to appear and then cut and eat. Not exactly. With such a short cropping season (six weeks in all), plants prone to slugs and snails, especially in our recent mild winters, the explosion of rabbits and wood pigeons, and the ever-present potential threat of asparagus flea beetle, life is not all a bed of roses. The good news, though, is that once established you can get up to 20 years of harvests from your crowns.

Vicky likes to save the thin weedy tips, called sprue, for soups and tarts, and boil the thicker spears and serve simply with melted butter. I prefer to chargrill from raw for about three to four minutes (medium/hot), and serve with Maldon sea salt, black pepper and a dash of lemon-infused oil or a good, sharp vinaigrette. Either is good, but remember, no overcooking otherwise you'll get a mushy result. Here is a delicious recipe for asparagus kindly given by Marlena Spieler, an accomplished and well-travelled chum from the chef world.

ROAST TRUFFLED ASPARAGUS WITH PARMESAN CHEESE

Pre-heat oven to 200°C/gas mark 6. Arrange the asparagus in a single layer in a shallow baking dish, sprinkle with olive oil then the salt and pepper. Place in the oven, and leave for about 7 minutes then remove and check to see its progress. The asparagus should be tender but still have bite. Toss with the garlic, then return to the oven for a few minutes longer, or until the asparagus is just crisp-tender. Garnish with the Parmesan cheese, letting it melt, then shake on a few generous drops of the truffle oil. Serve right away.

Serves: 4-6 (starter)
Preparation time: 5 minutes
Cooking time: 10 minutes

1 large bunch or 2 small/medium bunches asparagus★

3 tbsp extra virgin olive oil

Maldon salt and freshly ground black pepper, to taste

2 cloves garlic, chopped/crushed into a paste

5 tbsp freshly grated Parmesan★★

Several generous shakes of white truffle oil

★tough ends snapped off

★★or a well-matured cheddar from Denhay is very good

Smoking can be good for you

ONE OF THE recent concerns in the British food world has been the health benefits of eating particular foods. A well-known source of beneficial omega-oils is oily fish like herring, mackerel and salmon, and Patrick Gibb, proprietor of Bridfish Smokery, has charted the upturn in consumption. Having been in business over 30 years as a fish and meat smoker he is in a prime position to notice the changes in food fashions, and has seen a large trend towards fish generally, with kippers being his best-selling line. Originally a trout farmer at West Milton, in 1973 he decided to add value to his harvest and tried smoking some trout as an experiment; he has never looked back.

Smoking usually comprises two parts: cold and hot-smoking. It's a simple process. Oak sawdust is mechanically spooned onto hot plates, and the smoke created is drawn by fans into the smoke room, where the fish or meats are arranged in rows on metal racks. The initial smoking is for around 24 hours at ambient temperatures, and for larger cuts of fish like salmon steaks or chicken breasts there follows a period of some hours with the temperature turned up to about 90°C, cooking the product through, imparting oaky flavours without drying out the flesh.

Patrick has his processing and supply down to a fine art and tries wherever possible to source stock locally. Thus if you buy eels, mackerel or trout they are usually Dorset-caught, but obviously if you want salmon in quantity outside suppliers are necessary. His personal favourite is naturally-smoked haddock, without any of that yellow dye, along with mackerel. I urge you to try some smoked eel if you've never tried it – smoking elevates this lowly fish to gourmet status.

Brian Turner is one of Britain's most successful and well-known chefs and has some of the most respected restaurant names on his cv. Brian opened 'Turner's' in 1986 in Walton Street, Knightsbridge, and has become a successful television personality. He works hard for a number of charities with which he is involved and I am grateful for his gift here of a superb recipe that combines the robust flavours of fresh crab and smoked haddock.

CRAB AND SMOKED HADDOCK PASTIES

Sieve flour and salt into a bowl. Chop cold butter and lard into dice. Rub into flour to a sand-like texture. Use enough water to bring together as a dough, wrap in clingfilm and put in the fridge to rest for 30 minutes. Trim and chop spring onions then melt butter and sweat onions to soften on a medium heat. Take off the heat and allow to cool. Mix with cleaned and picked crab meats and flaked haddock then season with Tabasco, lemon juice and salt and pepper. Pin out the pastry, cut into 15cm circles, dust off excess flour then brush edges with beaten eggs. Place the mixed filling in the middle, 'pull up' the side and seal, crimping the edges tightly. Finally, brush with egg wash and bake in oven (180°C/gas mark 6) for 35-45 minutes.

Serves: 6
Preparation time: 50 minutes
Cooking time: 45 minutes

Shortcrust pastry:
450g plain flour
Pinch salt
120g lard
60g unsalted butter
145ml cold water
2 beaten eggs

Filling:
3 spring onions
30g butter
240g mixed crabmeat, cleaned and picked
120g smoked haddock★
Dash Tabasco pepper sauce
2 tbsp chopped chives
Squeeze of lemon juice
Salt and freshly ground black pepper

★My recommendation for a good fresh white fish supplier is MacSorsons trailer stall in Bridport's street market on Saturdays (usually on the north side, near the Post Office). The humble kiosk always has good crab meat, smoked undyed haddock, and a reasonably wide selection of white fish, reasonably priced. You have to get there early to ensure getting some – it's very popular!

Cream of the crop

THE YEAR IS 1988, the setting Lower Scoles Farm, 126 lush acres of green hillside in the beautiful Isle of Purbeck, directly opposite the ruins of Corfe Castle – where Peter and Hazel Hartle started Purbeck Ice Cream. When new milk quotas threatened the viability of the farm, they diversified into making their own ice cream rather than face over-production penalties. Creating a natural whole-milk product without any artificial colouring or additives, the couple built a business from a small cottage industry into one that now has a national distribution, and which has made them the proud winners of many awards. I asked Hazel if it had been a difficult start, and was surprised to hear they had some help in the shape of a course in ice-cream making, spotted in a farming magazine. Blackberry was their original flavour, as the fruit was literally on their doorstep. The first order was a batch of 10 tubs to the local garage, and since then they've never looked back.

The Purbeck brand has evolved offerings from the subtle and traditional through to the bold and exceptional. The core flavours of berry and clotted cream, vanilla, chocolate and toffee remain firm favourites, but add to these the sophisticated Spice Rack range, and you have grown-up appeal. No longer just a vehicle for a chewy pink wafer or a dribble of sticky red syrup, Purbeck Ice Cream has elevated this promenade favourite into the realm of the gourmet.

Here's a recipe that developed from my daydreaming about the tropics, attempting to turn a favourite tipple into a dessert. Use a standard alcohol gin (Bombay Sapphire is good) – the higher proof varieties won't freeze as easily.

Serves: 10
Preparation time: 10 minutes
Cooking time: 1 hour
10 minutes

16 medium egg yolks

200g vanilla sugar

1 litre rich double cream

400ml Schweppes tonic water

200g liquid glucose

75ml gin

GIN AND TONIC ICE CREAM

Beat yolks in a bowl and strain. Add sugar and beat until smooth and pale. Bring 500ml of cream to boil, add tonic, glucose and remove from heat. Whisk in sugar/egg mixture then simmer on very low flame, stir with wooden spoon until mixture has thickened to spoon-coating consistency. Remove from stove, add remaining cream to cool mix and arrest cooking process. Stir in gin and freeze in a plastic container. Refrigerate in deep-freeze (stir after 1 hour) until firm. Allow to warm up for 10 minutes for easy scooping.

Less is more

COMMERCIALLY-PRODUCED PASTA sauces can range from the gritty industrial-tasting Dolmio's (from a province of Italy, far, far away in Holland!), through the in-your-face appeal of the Loyd Grossman range, to Marks & Spencer's range, high class and authentic in taste but unfortunately not long-keeping, and so stuck on the chilled shelf. Which one to head for? Cue Simon Speight and Samantha Clarke of Lower Woolcombe Farm at Melbury Bubb, near Dorchester. Their *A Taste Of The Country* range has navigated their company, Rural Foods, through this tricky culinary minefield with unique sauce products that have both decent shelf-life and also hit the taste buds fair and square, made exclusively from homegrown Dorset tomatoes. Rural Foods was started by Sam and Simon to satisfy their desire for delicious food made from seasonal ingredients – on their 3-acre smallholding they grow fruit and vegetables as well as rearing sheep, pigs and chickens, farming with the least possible use of chemicals. Their current best-sellers are a range of traditional ice creams all made from local Dorset produce, they even make their own pasta, respected enough to be part of the serious offering from Manna Organic, as part of their pre-cooked range of frozen foods.

The sauces and dips arrive in plain glass jars with unfussy labels, and tied with raffia, and pasta in cellophane bags tied similarly (they wouldn't look out of place in a posh Italian deli). My preference is for quite robust, heavily-seasoned sauces and the range is unashamedly on the lighter side, but this is quite a deliberate move. On enquiry, Samantha kindly explains to me why home-made doesn't have to mean heavy-handed. They have a child who is lactose and gluten intolerant, so they started off being careful about what they were producing. No additives or preservatives, it was a case of 'less is more'. Simon assured me they get good feedback from customers, and sales figures bear out the fact that it suits customers to be able to find a sauce or ketchup that doesn't have sugariness or saltiness as standard. Like the pasta sauces, their ice cream has lower levels of sugar than much of the commercial competition. I tried their first flavour, gooseberry, and found it also a case of 'less is more' and as a result they have a very definite home-made feel to them.

So you can choose either style: Purbeck for full-on creamy impact or the lighter, home-made feel from Rural Foods.

Postscriptum: Simon and Sam's new organic vegetable boxes are going well. I can vouch for the top flavours – especially the sweet plums!

Passionate about purple

MARCH IS FIRMLY circled in my diary as the peak season for one
of the finest items in the seasonal noshing calendar – sprouting broccoli.
I daresay this noble purple-flowered spear would convert meat-heads
to veggie enthusiasts as much as the aroma of sizzling bacon has probably
broken the resolve of many a vegetarian.

Purple sprouting holds a special place in my heart as it was my first
taste epiphany experienced in my conversion to the gospel according to
Dorset. I took a stroll along Bridport's West Street market one Saturday
and came across one of the most elegant displays of prime quality fruit and
vegetables, that would have put any London market's produce to shame.
The Washingpool Farm sign gradually came to signify guaranteed quality.
The purpley, dark green spears seduced me with their firm freshly-picked
appearance and when I got home, I lightly steamed them with just a hint
of butter, a twist of salt and pepper. All that was needed. It was heavenly.
In fact, it was the catalyst in my resolve to finally move permanently to
the area… not house prices, the beautiful landscape or a school catchment
area… but this delicately-flavoured multi-speared verdant crown.

Washingpool's Farm Shop north of Bridport on the Salway Ash road
has become a one-stop shop for the best in Dorset, providing an outlet for
local suppliers as well as produce from their own 80-acre farm next door.
Growth of the shop has matched that of the Eveleigh founding family,
with four generations now living on the farm, and they are the first
associate members of Direct From Dorset's accreditation scheme.

Rest assured that Washingpool's seal of approval is firmly attached
to everything they display. Simon Holland and his family all share
one vision and their personal enjoyment of food translates into a quality
control that you can rely on – whether you're buying beef or biscuits.

Wyld about lamb

CLIVE AND JO Sage, owners and farmers of Wyld Meadow Farm near Charmouth, enjoy a prime position in a number of ways. First their land is some of the finest anywhere in Dorset, with good well-drained soil, some gentle valleys, and enough trees to provide a perfect balance for pasture and animals alike, between sunny exposure and shelter from the extremes of the elements. Second, the careful and dedicated husbandry of their Poll Dorset sheep and their Devon cattle has resulted in a top quality product with many awards for quality. So they join the ranks of the premier division producers like Manor Farm, Denhay and others who are fortunate to have a profile that extends beyond the county borders.

As a result of running the Bridport Farmers' market, Clive is very much in touch with what the consumer wants. Bridport's market is at the leading edge of popularity – as you would expect, with all the fine local producers to draw on for support – and there are at least 15 suppliers on the waiting list, as I write this. The powers-that-be seem to share this enthusiasm for Clive's efforts: Bridport Farmers' Market is being shortlisted currently for a DEFRA competition to find the best in the West.

Wife Jo is busy bringing up their two children, but still finds time to experiment with new recipes. Current best-selling lines include their spicy lamb-burgers with tomato, chilli and garlic, and the classic appeal of lamb sausages with rosemary. Their top-selling sausage with cranberry has won silver awards at Taste of The West competitions and they have gold for the last two years running for their leg of lamb and noisettes. Local chef Juliet Greener advises on new ideas, and of the telly chefs Jo admires Nigella Lawson, for her easy-to-achieve culinary style.

The Sages make a good team, and their fine lamb is admired by many including Phil Vickery, who cooked some Wyld Meadow breast of lamb to great acclaim for a West Country food promotion. Clive is conscious that the customer is somewhat more demanding (and enlightened) than in times gone by and shows a more adventurous spirit. Buyers ask questions and the Sages always find time to address these queries, and are happy to give advice on how to cook a particular cut or about animal welfare. As Clive says, if you trust the person selling it to you, you're more likely to have confidence in the product.

They treat their animals with the utmost respect, taking care to avoid stress right down to the final stages. To this end they are happy, along with many other farmers, to use Snell's abattoir at Chard. Clive notes that this respect pays dividends as animals that are roughly handled get stressed and change chemically, toughening the tissues – something that could defeat all the cautious husbandry up to that point.

Wyld Meadow have been selling direct for about 6 years now and they are proud to provide over 90% of their output for local sales. For the present, the Sages are very happy with the farm's progress, branching out to provide roe deer meat from their land, to be available for the local hotel trade, and in the future their small suckler cow herd will be expanded by cross-breeding their Devons with an Aberdeen Angus bull to provide a greater hardiness in the herd, and… I'm hoping… an even greater depth of beefy flavours.

As lamb of high quality abounds in the county, I have asked a good friend, Valentina Harris, one of the most noted authorities on Italian food and food culture, to suggest a dish that puts a modern Italian spin on an old classic. Valentina writes:

> This dish is faintly reminiscent of Boiled Mutton with Caper Sauce, which is one of those great British classics which for all sorts of reasons have recently become unfashionable. It strikes me that capers, which are used all over the Mediterranean and especially in southern Italian dishes, are actually very un-British in taste. I have opted for tender, pink chops instead of a somewhat tougher leg of mutton, bringing the dish firmly into this century. So when you make and taste the end result, I think you will find that the sour sauce cuts the sweetness of the lamb perfectly. Serve with boiled potatoes dressed with extra virgin olive oil.

LAMB CHOPS WITH A CAPER SAUCE

Light the grill to reach an even, medium heat. Rub chops all over with one of the garlic cloves and season them with salt and pepper. Now crush the remaining two garlic cloves – put them into a small frying pan with olive oil and anchovy paste. Fry together gently until garlic is completely softened. Add capers and stir together thoroughly. Dilute with wine and boil quickly for two minutes to evaporate alcohol. Simmer gently for 5 minutes, then taste and adjust seasoning. Bear in mind that capers tend to be very salty! If necessary, dilute with enough water to make up about one and a half tablespoons of sauce per chop. Keep warm until required. Grill the chops on both sides for about 5 minutes, or longer if you prefer them less pink. Arrange the chops on a warmed dish, sprinkle with the parsley and either cover with the sauce or serve the sauce separately.

Serves: 4
Preparation time: 5 minutes
Cooking time: 20 minutes

4 Barnsley chops★, trimmed

3 cloves garlic, peeled and finely chopped

2 tbsp extra virgin olive oil

½ tsp anchovy paste

4 tbsp capers (preferably salted) rinsed and dried, then chopped finely

½ glass dry white wine such as Frascati

1 tbsp chopped flat leaf parsley

salt and freshly ground black pepper

★A Barnsley chop is a double (ie. joined) chop across the saddle

Succulent seaweed

——

SAMPHIRE IS A sea vegetable that grows abundantly on muddy shorelines, marshy shallows and on salty mudflats. It has a crisp texture and tastes of the sea. This delicious tidal sea plant, often called sea-asparagus, grows in a limited number of places around the British coastline, and its true season is very short, lasting for about six weeks between mid-April to mid-June. To boost this, imports often come from parts of the coast of France and more recently, the Persian Gulf. Coastline effluent controls in the Middle East are less stringent than in the EEC and European samphire is a much safer bet as regards health and safety. If you are tempted to gather your own, bear sustainability in mind: if you snip a few bunches with a pair of scissors but avoid uprooting plants, as your ancestors have done since time immemorial, it's probably OK. You will also thus avoid a huge fine for harming the flora in a Site of Special Scientific Interest.

I hope that you understand my concern for our coastline. The fishing industry in places like the south coast is in decline and it is difficult to know whether you should be eating fish from the boats or not, given the dwindling state of the fish stocks. Obviously, some species are in greater difficulties than others and I will avoid, for example, recipes that use cod. I would rather be catching and cooking the fish myself, but if you are buying species like mackerel – still reasonably plentiful – straight from the seaside and cooking it at home, or eating fresh fish in a local restaurant, this is better than paying through the nose for an emaciated and disappointing farmed bass in a fancy city restaurant.

Do not overcook your samphire – it should retain its crunch. Any firm-fleshed fish will set off this taste-bud treat: it could be expensive sea bass, a more prosaic flat fish like brill, or the unattractive but tasty gurnard, a favourite choice in the county. In this case, the market that day supplied sea bream, which does the job nicely.

FILLETS OF SEA BREAM ON A BED OF MARSH SAMPHIRE

Bone out the two fillets, removing the skin (or ask your fishmonger to do it for you), and dust them with the seasoned flour. Heat frying pan with the oil on a medium-hot flame and then pan-fry each fillet for about 1-2 minutes on each side (don't overcook), drain dry on kitchen paper and keep warm while cooking the samphire. In a wok on a high flame, with a teaspoon of oil, stir-fry samphire in its own moisture with garlic and ginger until heated through. Add sesame oil and soy sauce. Continue to stir-fry for another couple of minutes tossing continuously. Finish off by adding the butter and taking off the heat. Swirl butter around to give it a shine, place portions on a warmed plate and arrange fish neatly on top.

Serves: 2
Preparation time: 15 minutes
Cooking time: 12 minutes

4 smallish or 2 medium fillets sea bream (say, 180g total weight per serving)

plain flour mixed with a heaped dsstsp medium-ground polenta and seasoned with fine sea salt and white pepper★

4 tbsp olive oil

360g samphire, cleaned and picked through

1 clove garlic, peeled and minced

1 small red chilli, deseeded, finely chopped

2cm piece root ginger, peeled, grated fine

a few drops sesame oil

1 tbsp light soy sauce

a small knob of unsalted butter

freshly ground black pepper (to serve)

★The addition of some cornmeal polenta to the dusting mix gives a texture with more bite

Back to school

THE PRETTY VILLAGE of Evershot is only a couple of miles from my own home. Residents are very lucky. It has several notable assets: attractive architecture, a luxury hotel (Summer Lodge), a top-notch pub with excellent food and rooms, and an artisan village bakery where you can taste delicious bread and cakes made in the traditional way. Tourists to this area bring home souvenir breads with the same fervour that Brits returning from an Italian holiday look forward to the fine olive oils from Tuscany. It is also home to celebrated chef Lesley Waters.

Lesley had a classical training, and made her mark at Prue Leith's restaurant following a spell of international cuisine in Germany in the late seventies. Lesley considers Prue ahead of her time in embracing the more ingredient-led simplicity of the Mediterranean cuisine. By the time Lesley had become a household name in the nineties through popular TV hits such as *Ready, Steady, Cook* they spent weekends in Dorset to escape the bustle of the capital. Lesley had done some filming in and around Dorchester and Sherborne, and loved the area. Time spent there became longer and longer and Lesley found herself starting her weekends on a Thursday and returning to the smoke on Tuesdays. She admits she found it the most beautiful place in the world and after a tough three years scuttling back and forth to London, decided to make the permanent leap, settling at The Old Manor in Evershot. Lesley's style of cooking had always been simple, using quality ingredients; she had found her spiritual home. Loving the local produce which she finds 'amazing', it was in her own words, 'the final piece in her jigsaw puzzle'.

After a few years of refurbishing the manor house to a new state of glory, Lesley started cooking demonstrations to great acclaim, and this has led to an expansion with new courses starting November 2005. The aims are to inspire and impart confidence to aspiring cooks of all levels, in a relaxed atmosphere, and naturally to use seasonal foods sourced locally, that Lesley finds are best. Lesley has perfected a simple but lush golden risotto that's perfect for a special supper.

SAFFRON RISOTTO WITH GARLIC BUTTERED SCALLOPS

In a large pan, heat the oil. Add the onion and cook for 10-12 minutes or until soft and golden. Stir in rice and cook, stirring for 1-2 minutes. Stir in the saffron and 1 ladleful of hot stock. Bring to the boil, and then reduce the heat to a simmer. As liquid becomes absorbed, gradually add more stock, a ladle at a time, allowing each ladle to be absorbed before adding the next, and stirring frequently until rice is cooked. Just before serving, heat half the butter in a frying pan. Add the scallops and cook quickly for 1-2 minutes, add the garlic and lemon juice and season with a little salt and black pepper. Finish the risotto with the remaining butter and cream and season to taste. Pile the risotto onto four plates or bowls, top with the scallops and serve at once with flat leaf parsley and lemon.

Serves: 4
Preparation time: 15 minutes
Cooking time: 25 minutes

1 tbsp olive oil

1 large onion, chopped

200g risotto rice

1½ tsp saffron (threads) infused in 2 tbsp boiling water

900ml (approx) hot vegetable★ or fish stock

30g unsalted butter

12 large scallops cleaned

1 clove garlic, crushed

juice of ½ lemon

100ml double cream

1 bunch flat leaf parsley

1 lemon, cut into wedges

Maldon salt and freshly ground black pepper

★Author's note: I would not be afraid to use a light chicken stock

Summer

—

West Bay
7 September 2004, 10.48am

Strawberry fields forever

I WAS SURPRISED one day to encounter a Liverpudlian selling strawberries at Beaminster's farmers' market, and wondered what he was doing down here – it was a bit of a leap from Penny Lane to Symondsbury, surely? Andy Brown worked in horticulture around the country then leapfrogged to fruit farming in Dorset with his family, and now supplies the local school children at Bridport County Primary with high-quality fruit, as well as farm shops and stalls hereabouts. I ask Andy for his favourite strawberry dish. Quick as a flash he grins: Eton Mess. But the best part? Mother-in-law does the picking!

Here's my take on the recipe. If you don't want the bother of making meringues from scratch use bought ones such as those found at Washingpool Farm Shop (which have a lovely slightly chewy centre), rather than mass-produced efforts that shatter to dust.

ETON MESS

Chop half the strawberries with icing sugar. Purée with the dessert wine, then pass through a fine sieve to remove seeds. Now halve the rest of the strawberries and whip the double cream to soft peaks. When ready to serve, place broken meringues in a large mixing bowl, add strawberries, and fold cream in and around. Then gently fold in all but about 2 tbsp purée to give a marbled effect. Finally, pile into a serving dish, spoon over the rest of the purée, and serve chilled.

Serves: 6
Preparation time: 25 minutes
Assembly time: 5 minutes

450g fresh strawberries, hulled and chilled

1 rounded tbsp icing sugar

3 tbsp sweet dessert wine (Beaumes de Venise/Vin Santo are good)

570ml organic double cream

6 meringues

Closed seasons

ACCORDING TO NORTH Sea fish population surveys by experts from the Centre for Environment, Fisheries & Aquaculture Science, nearly two thirds of species have moved further north as ocean temperatures rise. This is the first real scientific evidence of fundamental shifts as a result of rising temperatures. The movement is more dramatic than simple annual migrations and represents a firm link between distribution changes and global warming. Climatologists have issued dire predictions in the learned journal, *Science*, that if the trend continues, it may force some extinctions in some 40 or so years time. Not long in evolutionary terms.

Dave Park of Davy's Locker in Bridport has a large turnover of all types of fish and shellfish and supplies local pubs and restaurants as well as having a busy retail trade. It is this wide market that keeps his stock turnover fast and accordingly, I always trust the quality of all his produce. Dave has, as a fisherman and a dealer, years of experience with the fleet men who historically have ignored the warnings that catches must be regulated in order to ensure the viability of the industry. He said the fishermen are their own worst enemies – although to be fair, you can't criticise a man for doing his job efficiently. He suggested we should put a total ban on fish that are spawning – similar to the shooting season for game – to allow species to recover. Especially for the fish that have noticeably declined, like cod and monkfish. But if there is a unilateral stop for certain periods in the interest of ecology and conservation, could other countries be trusted to follow suit? Just look at the state of the Mediterranean. There's nothing left to eat there. Dave claimed to even have seen people netting out red mullets the size of a goldfish. Perhaps if we all obeyed new legislation for closed seasons, fish might just have a chance.

Given press reports of shoals of anchovies seen in waters as far north as Scotland, the waters off Dorset should also be seeing a shift in species, eventually reaching the fishmongers' slabs. The following recipe contributed by Sophie Grigson, food writer and broadcaster, may be perfect for Dorset.

MARINATED ANCHOVIES

Using a pair of scissors, snip off heads, tails and fins (don't forget the little dorsal fin on the back). Then cut down the belly and clean out the insides. Rinse with cold water. With a small knife, lengthen the cut down to the tail. Sit each one, cut side down, splayed out like butterfly, and press down on the back bone with the heel of your hand, flattening out the fish. Turn over and pick out the back bone. With scissors, cut off the ridge of small bones at the edges. Pat dry on kitchen paper. Spread them out skin-side up, in a shallow dish and sprinkle with a little salt between layers. Mix the vinegar with oil and pour over. Cover and leave for 8-24 hours in the fridge, turning occasionally. About 1 hour before serving, sprinkle with garlic and chives or parsley. Just before serving, scatter over the red pepper.

Serves: 4–6 (starter)
Preparation time: 45 minutes
Marinating time: 24 hours

450g fresh anchovies

salt

110 ml white wine vinegar
or rice vinegar

4 tbsp premium olive oil

1 clove garlic, finely chopped

1 tbsp finely chopped fresh
chives or parsley

¼ red pepper, very finely
chopped

THIS RECIPE IS courtesy of my great chums Chris and Carol Quayle's Auntie June. I had a fantastic snapper served in this novel style one memorable night chez Quayle, and begged the recipe, as it was such a different way to cook and serve a whole fish. The unusual sweet/sour combination is a variety of the traditional Portuguese/Spanish *escabeche*, or at least Auntie June's Jamaican take on it. Don't be frightened by the use of something as strong as vinegar in your cooking – just remember what's on the counter of every British fish 'n chip shop.

Fish is generally used for *escabeche*, occasionally chicken. First the fish is fried and placed in a dish large enough to hold all of the food in one layer. Then the marinade – usually made of onions, peppers, vinegar, and spices – is poured over the food while hot. The whole dish is then eaten hot or more often, allowed to rest overnight and served cold.

FISH ESCOVETCH

Choose a whole fish that meets all the necessary requirements to ensure freshness (ie. no sunken eyes, fishy smell, sticky gills etc.) then make criss-cross cuts on each side, dip in seasoned flour, then pan-fry until golden on both sides. Meanwhile, chop the onion, garlic, coriander, sweet red pepper, chillies, lemon and ginger. Blot excess oil off the fish with kitchen paper and rub the vegetable seasoning into the cuts, packing the remainder into the gut cavity for good measure. Place seasoned fish, in a foil-covered pan, into a preheated medium oven (190°C/gas mark 6/7) for 10 minutes or so, then remove foil and bake for another 10 minutes to get a crispy finish.

While it's cooking, chop onions, shallots and sugar into a saucepan with the white vinegar, bring to the boil, then take off heat so onions retain their crunch. Transfer the cooked fish to a suitable pre-heated serving dish and pour the vinegar/onion/shallot mixture over it. Garnish with coriander.

Serves: 4–6 (starter)
Preparation time: 20 minutes
Cooking time: 40 minutes

1 large whole fish, cleaned, gutted and scaled*

120g seasoned plain flour

Cooking oil (peanut is good)

Seasoning:

1 medium onion, finely chopped

4 cloves of garlic, finely chopped

1 handful chopped coriander

1 sweet red pepper, cored and finely chopped

2 medium-hot chillies, finely chopped

juice of 1 lemon

3cm piece of fresh ginger, finely grated

Marinade:

1 medium onion, peeled, finely chopped

6 shallots, peeled, finely chopped

1 tbsp caster sugar

2 glasses white wine vinegar

To serve:

handful fresh chopped coriander leaves

*A firm whole white fish, like sea-bass, gurnard, bream, hake or wrasse is fine. Soft varieties like whiting that break up during cooking are not suitable

Hotter than July

WEST BEXINGTON, NESTLING on the hillside en route to West Bay, is home to some of the hottest veg on the planet. At Sea Spring Farm Joy and Michael Michaud grow an amazing range of peppers and chillies, from mild to flaming hot, available fresh from July onwards mail order: Peppers By Post. I didn't readily associate peppers with the windy slopes of the Dorset coast, but protected from the fierce coastal storms by polythene tunnels the business is now in its tenth year. It's an exotic choice but the Michauds have been very successful, generally selling out of stock by December. People are getting to know more about chillies – recipes that used to say '1 green chilli' now often specify a particular variety. Michael, author of *Cool Green Leaves & Red Hot Peppers* (Frances Lincoln), endorses this. His book is sadly out of print now, but was ahead of its time in reflecting the current vogue for exotica and has great recipes and mouthwatering pictures.

One thing has puzzled me; when and how does a so-called sweet pepper get to be defined as a hot chilli? Joy explained: all peppers and chillies are from the capsicum family. Whether they are sweet, warm or hot varies according to the variety and the degree of physical heat they get from the sun. The catalogue lists many varieties and some new ones are grown every season – the latest addition being a mild(ish) habanero, available from a vivid lime green colour through yellow to an orangey-red. But be warned – the description 'mild' is only a relative term when applied to a habanero, as anyone who has tasted a Jamaican Scotch Bonnet will testify.

Finger lickin' good

I LOVE TO barbecue, especially with good charcoal like that made by the Dorset Charcoal Company. Chief and spokesperson Jim Bettle is proud of their success. The charcoal is made from sustainable wood coppiced locally, lights easily and quickly, and burns well to a good heat for grilling (with no noxious oily smoke like briquettes and thus no petroleum taint). Displaying the *Direct from Dorset* label that guarantees accreditation of origin, it costs a bit more than cheap garage forecourt imports but you are actually getting a first-class eco-friendly product and the best grilling ammunition around, as you need less of it to achieve the high heat needed.

These ribs, perfect for al fresco eating, go well with a fresh salad of seasonal leaves (Tamarisk Farm, Sunnyside, and Pat Foxwell's Ourganics are current favourites) and a good cold lager – try the Dorset Brewery's beers. If you want something non-alcoholic Dorset Blueberry Company's juice is great on the rocks and the Dorset Ginger Company's cordial with sparkling water is refreshing.

BARBECUE RIBS WITH BEER
After marinading overnight, roast in a low-medium oven (150°C/gas mark 2), uncovered (in the marinade) for about 1-1½ hours, turning the ribs frequently to avoid burning. When the meat shrinks away from the rib-bone slightly, it's done.

Take the ribs out and drain. Place the roasting tray on the hob over a high flame and reduce the sauce on a high heat until it's thick and treacly. The ribs can then be caramelised on the chargrill briefly, (about 3-5 minutes max) and served with the sauce poured over.

Try this dressing with a kick to go with your salad.

ROAST CHILLI DRESSING
Roast peppers and chillies on the chargrill (or in pre-heated oven – 250°C/gas mark 9) for 10-12 minutes to blister skins, then place in a bowl and sweat them under clingfilm until cool enough to touch. Peel, de-seed and core and process flesh on high speed with vinegar, lemon juice and oil, then adjust seasoning.

Peppers by Post (page 29) are a good source of peppers and chillies.

Serves: 4
Preparation time: min. 8 hours
Cooking time: 1¾ hours

About 3kg meaty pork spare ribs (cut in two)

soaked overnight in a marinade of:

350ml carton orange juice

70ml bottle soy sauce

juice of 3 lemons

4 tbsp brown sugar

1 small jar clear honey

4 cloves garlic, crushed

1 small bottle tomato ketchup

1 bottle beer eg. Tanglefoot by Badger Ales

⅓ small bottle 'Liquid Mesquite Smoke'

6cm piece fresh ginger root, finely grated

1 tsp chinese 5 spice powder or 3 star anise

1 tbsp hot pepper sauce

Preparation time: 5 minutes
Cooking time: 20 minutes

4 green/red peppers ('Hungarian Hot Wax')

3 hot red chillies ('Cherry' is good for this, or 1 habanero)

1 tbsp wine/balsamic vinegar★

juice of 1 lemon

6 tbsp virgin olive oil

Maldon salt and freshly ground black pepper

★Merchant Gourmet's oils and vinegars are good for dressings

Live yoghurts

WOODLANDS PARK DAIRY, run by Richard and Reita Murray, produces sheep and goat yoghurts from milk supplied by local herds. Sheep's milk has a greater benefit as regards nutrition with higher calcium levels and minerals, but there has always been a kind of prejudice because of the sourness of the sheep's milk and the 'farmyardy-goat' aroma of goats' milk. I personally like the sharp tang associated with the former, and the extreme 'goatiness' of the latter has been reduced by clever selection of the milk at source. Reita informed me that not all breeds of goat have the same strength of milk, and of course diet plays a large part.

They make a range of yoghurts with soft fruits, cherry, apricot, strawberry and blackcurrants, that allow the consumer an easy introduction to good alternatives to cows' milk products. I particularly like the natural goats' milk yoghurt and add my own fruits in season, with a little honey or maple syrup. Woodlands Park Dairy has been organically registered for a number of years now, and they have won Best Organic Product from The West Country Food Awards and 1st, 2nd and 3rd places at The Bath & West Show. Their yoghurts have good shelf life as regards the 'bio' element – up to 28 days – and Reita points out their Woodlands live culture has been proven to endure successfully beyond that. They plan to try a new variety using blueberries supplied by David Trehane of the Dorset Blueberry Company.

I've found my thrill

—

WHY IS IT that so many of the things I really like to consume without caution (like *fois gras*, roast potatoes in goose fat, red meat and cheese), all seem to have a warning attached to them? Well, at last I've found a truly more-ish thing that actually does you good. Blueberries are the healthiest fruit you could eat. It's official. Recent studies are hailing the fruits and their juice as the best of antioxidants, disease fighters that also help slow down the outward and inward effects of ageing. They're full of vitamin C, are great for digestion, and it's rumoured they're even able to enhance your love life!

The Dorset Blueberry Company at Wimborne takes advantage of the acidic soil found in parts of the county, favoured by rhododendrons and also by bilberries, the wild antecedent of the cultivated commercial blueberry (genus Vaccinium). Although called blue, nature does not produce much in the way of true blue pigments and the juice is more of a dark bluey/red-purple. The colour, and the beneficial antioxidant properties, are actually due to organic chemicals called anthocyanosides.

So much for the science bit, what about the taste of blueberry juice? Take it from me – it's great. It has far more concentrated vitamin C than most cranberry juices on the market today and has no added water, just 25% apple juice to take the edge off the acidity. One of the best ways of adding these antioxidants to your diet is by simply drinking the juice. Sweet and fruity enough to chug down, but with a hint of tartness that's refreshing. Try it on its own, or it's great as a cocktail with champagne, with vodka and ice, or spritzed up with sparkling spring water.

Blueberries are great for baking too.

BLUEBERRY AND PECAN LOAF

Sprinkle 2 tsp flour over the blueberries. Sift remaining flour with sugar, baking powder and salt. Stir in oats. Blend eggs, butter, syrup, vanilla and mashed banana. Combine with dry ingredients. Stir in pecans and ground almonds. Fold in blueberries. Pour into buttered and floured loaf tin. Bake in hot oven (180°C/gas mark 4) for 1 hour. Let cool 10 minutes. Remove from pan. Cool before slicing.

Serves: 8
Preparation time: 20 minutes
Cooking time: 1 hour

120g fresh blueberries

360g sifted self-raising white flour

150g organic caster sugar

1 tbsp ground almonds

2¼ tsp baking powder

½ level tsp salt

120g fine rolled oats

2 medium eggs, beaten

1 tbsp golden syrup

6 tbsp melted butter

1 tsp vanilla extract

1 small mashed ripe banana

120g chopped pecans

Beating the French

———

GREAT BRITAIN NOW has more regional varieties of cheese than France. Cranborne Chase Cheese have two good new(ish) cheeses – St. Nicholas, a small soft creamy cheese with a crinkly soft crust, and Win Green, a soft rind cheese similar to Camembert. Both are made from unpasteurised milk, which is divine for the cheese lover and hell for the Environmental Health Officers, but cheesemaker Richard Biddlecombe was only complimentary about the EHOs as they have organised specialist cheese courses on the best methods to maintain hygiene. The owners of the farm, Peter and Priscilla Kininmouth, are rightly proud of these cheeses that give the French a run for their money.

Cheeses are runnier in winter as the feed of the cows change – the fat content is higher and it's colder so the whey juices don't drain so readily. Summer cheeses benefit from fresh-flavoured milk from lush pasture, but have lower fat which makes them drier and hence harder. Richard acknowledges that the customer understands more now than ever before and sees the benefits of buying locally. But there is one area he still worries about. Do the English really know how to keep the cheese? All too often we serve soft cheeses early, and straight out of the fridge. We still need to grasp the need and importance for ripening.

Meanwhile, try slicing off the crust/lid of a cold, ripe Win Green (straight from the fridge), spooning on some Dorset Blueberry Company's spiced blueberry sauce, replacing the 'lid' and bake in a hot oven (180°C/ gas mark 4) for 5 minutes. Then dip/spoon on crusty bread. Mmmm.

Hidden depths

——

EX-ROYAL NAVY diver Darren Brown makes his living from the seabed, scooping up primarily scallops, and anything that wanders into his mask's field of vision, like lobsters, crabs and flatfish. Darren is fastidious about the care and transport of his harvest and reserves his loudest curses for the practice of seabed dredging, something that wreaks havoc with the environment as everything is hoovered up. Dredging for scallops is indiscriminate and kills up to 15 species to get at the shellfish, with the seabed taking years to recover. Darren is appalled; 'they're cutting down the apple trees to collect apples'. He is a 'hands-on' boss and dives with his team of two for about 1½ hours twice a day, selecting scallops by hand and eye. Small ones are left to maintain the population and adult shells are graded from 100mm (small), 105mm (medium) to 120mm (large). Darren recommends mediums – they are a good size but have the sweetest flavour.

Previous page: Scallop diver (and ex–Royal Marine) Darren Brown brings in his catch

Darren's wife, Jo, is part of the Shellseekers team, and brings produce from the holding tanks to the kitchen for cleaning. Crabs, prawns and their famous scallops are prepared here and stored for distribution. Scallops benefit from being deep-water molluscs. The potential for contamination that threatens the purity of surface shellfish like mussels and oysters doesn't affect them as pollution passes over harmlessly.

Shellseekers supply a couple of high-profile chefs: Jamie Oliver and Mark Hix, but otherwise the bulk of their business is via Borough Market, in London, recently twinned with La Boccaria in Barcelona. They sell about 100 dozen or so scallops a week and at peak may ship 500-600 dozen to London markets, where they can, sadly for us, fetch a price double that of local Dorset sales.

Throw them back – into the pot!

MARK HIX IS one of the leading lights of modern british cuisine.
He is the Chef Director of Caprice Holdings Ltd, overseeing Le Caprice,
The Ivy and J. Sheekey, some of London's most fashionable restaurants.
He grew up in the Bridport area and I am grateful for his recipe
contribution below for spider crab taken from his latest book *Fish, etc.*
Mark writes: 'If only I knew what I was doing as a kid, throwing those
ugly looking spider crabs out of my prawn net and back into the water.
We don't use spider crab much here but in Spain it's a delicacy and that's
where I came across a dish very similar to this. You can use ordinary
brown crab in this dish, but if you do come across spider crabs, buy
them, as the meat is sweet and worth the trouble'.

This is easier than it seems – it just takes time. Be patient. It will
pay dividends.

SPICED BAKED SPIDER CRAB

To get crab meat out, twist legs and claws off, then crack them open
with the 'back' of a stout knife and remove the white meat. Now turn
the main body on its back and twist off the pointed flap. Push the tip
of a table knife between the main shell and the bit to which the legs
were attached and twist the blade to separate the two, then push it up
and remove. Scoop out the brown meat in the well of the shell and put
with the leg and claw meat. On the other part of the body remove the
dead man's fingers (these are the feather-like, grey gills attached to the
body) and discard. Split the body in half with a heavy knife. Now you
need to be patient and pick out the white meat from the little cavities
in the body. Add this to the rest of the meat.

Gently cook the onion, garlic, ginger and chilli in 10ml of the olive
oil until soft. Add the sherry, fish stock and brown crab meat, stir well
then add most of the breadcrumbs (reserving a few to scatter on top),
half the lemon juice and season to taste. Simmer for 15 minutes stirring
occasionally. Blend one-third of the mix with the rest of the olive oil
in a blender, then stir it back into the mixture along with the spider-crab
meat. Add more lemon juice and seasoning if necessary. Spoon the
mixture back into the shells or an ovenproof serving dish and scatter
the rest of the breadcrumbs on top. Lightly brown under the grill or
in a hot oven. Serve with thin slices of toast.

Serves: 4 (starter)
Preparation time: 25 minutes
Cooking time: 35 minutes

1 large (1½-2kg) spider crab,
cooked

100g extra brown crab meat

half onion, peeled, finely
chopped

1 clove of garlic, peeled, crushed

10g knob of ginger, scraped,
finely chopped

½ small mild chilli, de-seeded,
finely chopped

110ml olive oil

40ml sherry

50ml fish stock (a good stock
cube will do)

juice of ½ lemon

50g fresh white breadcrumbs

Maldon salt and freshly ground
black pepper

This is a soup that can be served in a small bowl as a starter or in a large bowl as a satisfying main course. Like most oriental cooking it is fairly quickly made (once preparation is complete), and can be cooked in one pot. The ingredients listed below are an ideal wish list but the idea is that you use whatever is good and available in the market that day. Crab is great, langoustines are fantastic (if pricey). Try to use white fish that will keep its firmness and not disintegrate eg. monkfish is better than whiting. Mussels are optional, but add a great deal of impact taste-wise and are inexpensive.

SEAFOOD LAKSA SOUP
In a large saucepan, sauté chopped onion (high flame) until edges of the onion turn brown. Then add stock, laksa paste and coconut milk (including creamy residue) then bring to the boil (if mussels are available add the strained cooking juices). Whisk together until incorporated and add grated ginger and garlic. Remove from heat. Next, gut and clean squid, cut into 6cm rectangles and criss-cross pieces on inside surface, add to soup with noodles, fish chunks, and prawns (if prawns are cooked already, add later) and simmer 3-4 minutes until noodles are soft. Add beansprouts and coriander leaf (cooked prawns here), check seasoning and serve with a few spring onions scattered over. This soup is best eaten with chopsticks and a spoon.

LAKSA PASTE
Blend the dry, hard (coriander seeds, nuts, dried shrimp, pepper etc.) ingredients first, then add the oil and the softer ingredients (lemon grass, onion, sugar, spices, garlic etc.) until smooth and then add leafy stuff (lime zest, leaves, juice). Blend until all consistent red colour and store in the fridge in a screw-top jar. It will keep for 3 weeks or so before losing potency.

Serves: 4–5
Preparation time: 25 minutes
Cooking time: 20 minutes

1 tbsp laksa paste (see recipe following)

1 medium onion, peeled, medium chopped

1 tbsp peanut oil

450ml strong chicken stock (see recipe on page 60)

400ml can coconut milk (full fat creamy top reserved)

3cm piece peeled ginger root, finely grated

1 clove garlic, peeled, pulped

30g vermicelli-style rice noodles

small bunch laksa leaves, stalks removed

30g fresh Chinese-style beansprouts

Maldon salt and freshly ground black pepper

1 bunch spring onions (with green 'flags'), roughly chopped

Fish:

3 small squids, fresh if possible

60g fresh prawns, de-shelled

60g fresh white fish fillets (firm flesh preferred)

60g fresh mussels (cooked, de-shelled, juices reserved)

To garnish/serve: a couple of cooked large prawns, head off but tail-end shell on, split lengthways

Preparation time: 15 minutes

This Malaysian–style paste is spicy but not red–hot like Thai/Burmese

6 tbsp peanut oil

3 cloves garlic, peeled

1 tbsp coriander seeds

3 medium hot chillies, seeds included

1 tsp paprika

1 tsp cumin

1 small shallot

½ tsp black pepper

1 tsp turmeric

zest and juice of 1 lime

1 tsp shrimp paste

3 tbsp dried shrimp

30g Macadamia nuts

5 or 6 stalks lemon grass, tough outer leaves removed

1 tbsp soft brown sugar

3cm piece of fresh galangal, peeled, grated fine

small bunch laksa leaf (called *pael* in Thai and *Dao Kasom* in Malay) coriander leaf will do as a substitute

Heaven scent

BIODYNAMIC FARMING DUO Ian and Denise Bell follow the principles
set out by philosopher Rudolf Steiner in the 1920s. Working with the
seasons and the solar and lunar calendars, it is a holistic approach to
farming. For some, who see only an esoteric philosophy, it is more a leap
of faith than a way of life – but whatever their feelings about this farming
technique it certainly pays dividends. Heritage Prime produce is favoured
by a strong client list that includes, amongst others, Michel Roux, Nigella,
Jamie and Hugh. I myself have joined the ranks of the converted, and can
say with hand on heart that Shedbush produce some of the most awesome
meat (and eggs!) I have ever tasted. So whatever Denise and Ian are doing –
they really are on the right track!

Heritage Prime can offer you biodynamic meat, full-flavoured
beef or my favourite, Tamworth pork, produced to the highest organic
standard (Demeter certification 331). Eggs (chicken, duck or the very
fine turkey eggs) are sold at the gate – but ring first to get an appointment.

I'm very grateful to the Bells for donating their kitchen secrets to
Eat Dorset. Denise writes:

> Over the years, this recipe has been much enjoyed and adapted by many chefs
> and food writers. From the Shedbush farmhouse kitchen this recipe ensures
> guaranteed lazy successful feasting – just let the quality of the pork do the work!
> The fine Tamworth pigs' shoulders weigh about 9 to 10 kilos, coming from slowly
> matured pigs of about 18 months to 2 years of age. (Most pigs are killed at around
> 4 months.) It is the very high quality and careful rearing of our meat that makes
> this dish so delicious and good for you.

THE ORIGINAL HERITAGE PRIME SLOW-ROASTED SHOULDER OF PORK

The meat will take 24 hours to cook (7–8 hours for a half shoulder) and will fill your home with a wonderful meaty ambience. Let's assume that you want to eat this for Sunday lunch; you'll need to start thinking of switching on your oven at about lunchtime on Saturday. Use a stout roasting vessel, preferably cast iron. Take half of the salt, sprinkle all over the skin and massage this well into the skin and into scored tissue for a good 3–4 minutes so that the heat and action of your hand begins to 'melt' the salt. Gently pour olive oil over the shoulder rubbing in as you do so. Next, add the remaining salt to black pepper and the thyme in a bowl, mix thoroughly and sprinkle evenly over the pork.

Muster all your strength to lift the dish into a hot oven and leave 30 minutes. Then remove it from the oven and lower temperature (to 140°C/gas mark 1). Baste with a large spoon for 2 minutes and return joint to low oven and ignore it for 23 hours.

About half an hour before you plan to eat, turn up oven to 220°C/gas mark 7, to ensure sublime crackling. At this point, pop apples around the pork, tucking under where possible. Then remove from oven, pull off the crackling, and carve – or even tear the meat away with a fork. Serve with organic roast potatoes and steamed dark green cabbage tossed in butter, seasoned with plenty of black pepper.

Serves: 15–20
Preparation time: 15 minutes
Cooking time: 24 hours

1 whole shoulder of Heritage Prime Tamworth pork, skin scored diagonally★

4 tbsp organic olive oil

1 tbsp coarse freshly ground black pepper

1 tbsp Maldon sea salt

wild or garden thyme (including flowers if in flower)

6 organic orchard apples

★A half shoulder from one of the Bells' pigs feeds 8–10 people

Above: Garlic slow-roasted loin of Heritage prime pork

Smoke 'em if you've got 'em

I AM LUCKY to have an outdoor chargrill that has an oven compartment underneath. It can roast a joint of meat, or with the addition of wet woodchips over a small pile of hot charcoal can smoke meat or fish. Speed of cooking can be adjusted by varying the charcoal source of heat, and I can achieve a well-smoked chicken by slow smoking (keep topping up the woodchips) over a 2-2½ hour period rather than just a quick roast for 1½ hours at a higher temperature. The picture on opposite shows a wild-garlic-stuffed chicken getting the smoky oven treatment. It can be eaten hot or cold. I am grateful to Andrew Barshall for suggesting this brunch dish is robust enough to include in *Eat Dorset*.

SMOKED CHICKEN HASH

Wash and boil the potatoes for about 7-9 minutes depending on size until cooked through (*al dente* in the centre). Drain, then refresh in cold water. Allow to cool, then peel (discard skins), chopping into small chunks (no bigger than 2cm). Shred the meat into medium shreds (with skin) and fry in 1 tbsp of the oil for a couple of minutes over a hot flame to heat and sizzle, but not long enough to dry out the meat. Add the spring onions and cook a minute then add the other spoonful of oil and the knob of butter and the cooked potatoes. Allow to colour up golden brown around the edges, shaking the pan to agitate the spuds to evenly distribute the browning process.

Meanwhile, heat your grill to maximum. Sprinkle with salt and a few twists of black pepper and a shake of parsley. To plate up, divide the pan mix into two plates, place a soft-poached egg on top of each and spoon over the hollandaise to cover the egg, then flash under the hot grill for a couple of minutes until the sauce is just about to brown up in patches. Devour with gusto and a piece of toast to sweep the plate clean of yolky sauce.

Serves: 2
Preparation time: 15 minutes
Cooking time: 35 minutes

250g cold smoked chicken

4 spring onions, medium chopped

2 tbsp virgin olive oil

350g pink fir apple or other salad potatoes

small knob of unsalted butter

2 poached eggs

4 tbsp hollandaise sauce

Maldon sea salt and freshly ground black pepper

2 tbsp flat leaf parsley, finely chopped

Living the dream

IF YOU WANT exotic salads, you should go to Patricia Foxwell of Ourganics. Ourganics lies on (almost) level clay land between Litton Cheney and Burton Bradstock. 9 acres of old water meadow have been transformed by Pat into a mini Garden of Eden using a plan-for-living called permaculture. Traditional English vegetables are no problem and Pat also grows herbs and exotic salad varieties, using companion planting for phyto-protection against would-be predators. Permaculture enables a degree of self-sufficiency with all natural materials being provided by the immediate locale and no food miles involved, or indeed, any other miles of any sort, minimising the impact on the environment.

The clay soil is mineral-rich but needed fibrous organic matter to break up the texture. Compost is created and matured. A keen practitioner of the greenest eco-friendly type of garden husbandry, she has arranged her entire series of raised bed growing areas to be cleverly irrigated by a series of channeled streams, controlled by bungs and overflow pipes, fed by gravity from a spring in the village 1 mile away. This is vital for time-saving during her working day otherwise her daily watering regime alone would take at least 5 hours. High hedges, both maintained and natural, afford protection from wind and dotted about are netted igloo-shaped frames that keep birds and other predators off the more delicate crops. Spring and November/December are peak harvest times for Pat, and gluts of fruit are bottled efficiently. Plans are afoot for wild cherries, crab-apples and more herbs to increase the large range of fruits and vegetables currently in her collection. To expand the exotic herb range new varieties of seeds like Mibuna, turnip greens, Tatsoi, Par-cel and Red Perilla are being readied for next season's offerings, which she is happy to deliver personally – loving the opportunity to show her produce to best effect.

The overall impression is one of abundance, with sculpture, an open-air hot tub, water butts, piles of logs, chickens running about, open fires and cooking pots lending a rustic charm without any whiff of contrivance, because you know Pat wholeheartedly believes in what she is doing and leads only by example – her motto being 'Earthcare, Fairshare, People-Care'. Her idea of luxury is a cold water tap with running water. She has a blindingly optimistic vision, believing that what others consider problems, are opportunities of finding another way forward. Holistic husbandry, creating shelter with minimum impact, eating seasonally and sharing knowledge are her achieved objectives. Future plans? A Welsh cob to make deliveries to customers.

Unlike other more aggressive farming regimes, who aim to build an empire they can bequeath to their children, Pat's testament will be her own way of life. She will have left no footprint behind, nor any trace of damage to the earth that sustained her. It's a green fantasy that she has realised in her own lifetime. As Pat enthuses – 'It's totally absorbing and very hard work. But it's very rewarding'.

Dairy made

I REPRODUCE A recipe below for a raspberry tart that's always easy and gives an impressive result. Originally designed to use a rich Italian mascarpone, I adapted it for the lushest cream I've enjoyed in Dorset, the gorgeous, yellow, thick organic Jersey cream from Tim and Julie Garry's Jersey herd at Modbury Farm near Burton Bradstock. They also farm saddleback pigs – not an easy task in winter due to the heavy clay ground, but it's the cream that knocks my socks off. Tim and Julie are rightly proud of their organic herd's output and boast that their milk is real milk, that lasts, and it has 15% more calcium content than average. They can sell you milk unpasteurised if you like, but sales are only available via the gate, due to environmental health restrictions. The herd continue to grow from strength to strength and the 3 separate 'families' of handsome Jersey cows that make up their total enjoy a status at Modbury equal to most house pets, with daily contact giving way to a affectionate relationship that is mutual and demonstrative.

RASPBERRY, ALMOND AND JERSEY CREAM TART

Grease the springform tin with oil and a piece of paper kitchen towel. Line with a circle of baking parchment cut out to fit the bottom and sides, to ease out the finished base when baked and cooled. In a mixing bowl beat together the butter and sugar until creamy and then add half the nuts, then the remainder by degrees. You should be aware that this recipe can be made only by sight, ie. the given volumes of butter and sugar, and then enough ground almonds to end up with dough that does not feel greasy or sticky.

You won't be able to roll this paste so simply push a layer down onto the bottom of the tin (lined with parchment) 5mm thick and prick all over with a large fork to stop the pastry 'ballooning' when baking. Place in a hot oven (200°C/gas mark 6) for 12-15 minutes, on the middle shelf and check that the pastry does not burn but has coloured up slightly to a golden-brown hue. Allow to cool completely.

Meanwhile whisk liqueur into the cream until thickened and when the base is completely cold unclip the side(s) and spread the cream mix onto the almond base and smooth out with a palette knife until completely level, then place fruits decoratively around the outside curve working your way into the middle keeping the fruits tight up to one another. Make a glaze by boiling the seedless jam with the lemon juice and allow to cool for 5-10 minutes then brush over the fruits to seal them with a soft pastry brush. Chill in the fridge 15 minutes to set the glaze, and serve.

(Remember when cutting to allow for the paper disc underneath.) This only keeps for some 6 hours before the fruit juices leak out and make the pastry soggy so don't keep it too long!

Serves: 2
Preparation time: 15 minutes
Cooking time: 15 minutes
Assembly time: 35 minutes

You will need a 25cm springform tin for baking the base, and strong baking parchment

1 tsp sunflower (or other bland) oil

150g organic salted butter, softened

110g organic caster sugar

about 225g ground almonds

2 tbsp liqueur of choice★

500g Modbury organic double cream

900g fresh firm raspberries

1 x 350g jar seedless raspberry jam

juice of 1 freshly squeezed lemon

★I used home-made blueberry vodka, a kind gift from Oakland's Plantation, with my raspberries but use your imagination to combine fruits with liqueur cream to enhance the effect. I have used good Crème de Mure and Cassis in the past successfully. Grand Marnier with strawberries works well

The gold standard
——

THE NATURE OF hive honeys varies according to the aromas occurring in each flower species in the locale. Most people have tasted the extremes of character from the pale, mild acacia flower honey, through the medium heather honeys of moorland to the resinous gum tree honeys of Australia and the strong, dark mountain honeys of the Greek mountainsides, redolent of wild thyme and oregano. Dorset flora gives a mild to medium flavour, which is fine for pouring onto natural unflavoured yoghurt or spreading on bread. Although different styles of honeys are abundant from the commercial producer, overall yields are small in the county and much comes from gifted amateurs. Many honey producers are aware that demand outstrips supply, even on a worldwide scale, and Dorset is no exception.

Sometimes I adapt local honey for recipes that require a more robust honey flavour, by bubbling the honey in a saucepan, reducing it and condensing the character to a more full-on level. Going beyond this point reduces the syrupy honey to a darker point where it becomes caramelised and has that almost bitter-sweet taste you associate with crème caramel pudding. Below is a related recipe that is great for a smooth textured finale to a summer dinner, that can be made in advance, to allow you more time for your dinner guests. It was inspired by Bruce Jones, a gifted cook and friend I have cooked with over many years.

BAKED CUSTARDS WITH VANILLA AND CARAMELISED HONEY

Preheat the oven to 160°C/gas mark 3. Combine cream, milk, honey with vanilla pod in a saucepan and heat to near simmer. Allow to cool and infuse. Whisk eggs/yolks in a bowl. Pick out vanilla pod from cream mixture and pour half of this cooled, infused mixture onto the eggs and whisk well then add remainder and combine. Strain through a fine sieve to remove threads or bits and pour into 6 lightly buttered ovenproof ramekins or custard cups. Place foil over each top and place in a hot water *bain-marie*, the water reaching halfway up the ramekin sides. Bake for about 30 minutes until just set. Don't overcook as the latent heat residual in each cupful will continue to set the custard mix.

Allow to cool, then remove foil (with excess condensation attached on the underside), then clingfilm and chill in the fridge for 2-3 hours before serving.

For the syrup, boil the honey quite fiercely in a saucepan and reduce until quite dark to a thick caramel, stirring occasionally to prevent sticking and burning. Remove from the heat allow to cool down for 5 minutes then add the water. Mix through and allow to cool to room temperature. To serve, dip each cup base briefly into hot water to melt the buttered seal and unmould the custard, then turn out upside down onto the serving plate and pour the caramelised honey over.

Serves: 6
Preparation time: 1 hour
Cooking and chilling time: 3 hours

Custard:
40ml single organic cream
200ml whole organic milk
1 fresh vanilla pod, split
75g honey
2 medium organic eggs
3 medium egg yolks
unsalted butter – to grease ovenproof ramekins/cups

Syrup:
150g honey
3 tbsp water

Autumn

___

The master butchers

A REAL MASTER butcher's shop means somewhere they know the provenance of their meat, hang it properly, know the cuts, and understand customers' demands. My personal favourite happens to be England's oldest family butchers R J Balson & Son, at the west end of Bridport, where Richard, the latest scion of this meaty heritage, keeps the flag flying for traditional meat and game. Not that they have stood still by any means. Twenty years ago you would only have been able to buy pork or beef sausages here. Now the customer demands more choice and they stock many varieties including award-winning pork and mustard, wild boar and genuine Toulouse. I can vouch for its authenticity, coarse ground and garlicky.

Richard is rightly proud of his quality control: he sources his lamb, pork and cracking good beef from respected local farms, and he can supply you with, say, a pheasant that has been hung for exactly your preferred time. Don't miss his pickles, pies, black puddings, faggots and brawn as well as the top (award-winning!) dry-cure smoked bacon in Dorset.

BREAST OF PHEASANT WITH PORT AND ORANGE

Cut the breasts (removing skin) neatly from each carcass and set aside. Chop carcasses into small pieces, roast in a hot oven (220°C/gas mark 7) for 15-20 minutes. Then place the browned bones in a large saucepan with veal and chicken stocks, along with the port, juice and peel. Bring to the boil, simmer for 30 minutes skimming off any froth, then decant through a muslin/very fine sieve into a saucepan (discarding all the bones and bits). Cook on a high heat until the liquid has reduced by about two-thirds. This will form the basis of your gravy-cum-sauce.

Next, season each breast lightly (easy on the salt) and stretching each rasher thinly lengthways with the back of a knife, wrap each breast around to form a bacon overcoat. Roast the breasts (200°C/gas mark 6) in a 5mm layer of reduced stock to prevent the meat burning and sticking. This will take from 20-30 minutes (test it by removing and prodding with your finger for rareness – it should hopefully have some give). Then lift out and keep warm. Add remaining stock and redcurrant jelly to the *jus*, pour over the meat, and serve with braised Savoy cabbage and potatoes.

Serves: 4
Preparation time: 1 hour
Cooking time: 35 minutes

2 pheasants

120ml veal stock★

300ml chicken stock★

120ml robust port

juice of ½ orange

peel of ⅓ orange

Maldon salt and freshly ground black pepper

8 Denhay smoked streaky bacon rashers

1 tsp redcurrant jelly

★See stock recipes on page 84

A food lover

HENRIETTA GREEN HAS been one of the catalysts for the dramatic changes that have taken place in Britain's gastronomic culture over the last 10 years. Author of *The Food Lovers Guide* and tireless organiser of Food Lovers Fairs, she exhorts us to support local producers, as it is important not only in order to find food with real taste and flavour, made with real ingredients and in the proper way, but also to support our small speciality farmers and growers.

When she started working on her first *Food Lovers Guide*, she actually wondered whether there was a market for that kind of book, because food was not as important a part of British culture as it is of European culture. Fortunately that has changed, not least thanks to her contribution. Henrietta has kindly given her support to *Eat Dorset* with this guest recipe, and her thoughts below about gathering wild fungi.

> For the first hour on my first-ever hunt, I hardly spotted a mushroom even though my eyes were firmly glued to the ground. Then I observed, discreetly at a distance, of course, (some mushroom hunters are territorial and jealous, solitary creatures) a well-seasoned Italian. Poking here, peering there, she knew how to look, how to let shapes and colours fall into place and she knew where and what to look out for. Soon my own basket was filling with the odd *Russula* or slippery Jack and I was away. And since then and over several years, I have gathered all the usual suspects – parasols, puff-balls, blewits, black trumpets, honey fungus, chicken o' the woods, even ceps.

MUSHROOM AND BUTTERBEAN SOUP

Place mushrooms in a bowl; pour over 300ml boiling water and leave to soak for 30 minutes or until mushrooms are soft. Using a slotted spoon lift out the mushrooms and refresh in cold water, reserving the mushroom's soaking water. In a large saucepan, heat olive oil, add onion and garlic then cook gently over a moderate heat for 5-7 minutes. Drain butter beans and add, stirring with a wooden spoon until well coated with olive oil. Then pour in 700ml of water and the reserved mushroom water, gently bring to the boil and simmer for 90 minutes or until beans are completely soft. Blitz the soup until it is smooth. Return to the pan, stir in yoghurt, adjust seasoning and gently re-heat. If you like your soup with a bit of texture, keep a few whole beans back before you purée the soup, then stir them in with the yoghurt. Meanwhile, melt the butter in a suitable sauté pan. Roughly chop the mushrooms, add to the pan and sauté gently for 5 minutes or until tender. Stir into the soup, adjust seasoning and sprinkle over chopped parsley before serving.

Serves: 4–6
Preparation time: 30 minutes
Cooking time: 1 hour 40 minutes

30g dried wild mushrooms★

2 tbsp olive oil

1 onion, sliced

2 cloves garlic, crushed

500g butter beans, soaked overnight in water

700ml water

150ml full fat Greek-style yoghurt

30g butter

salt, freshly ground pepper

freshly chopped parsley

★Make sure your mixture is a varied one; ideally it should include at least a few slices of ceps as these have the best body and a deep beefy flavour

John Wright leads a fungus foray at the Kingcombe Centre

Wild fungi abound in our countryside; but it's not safe to guess
a species looks right, you have to be sure. I sought the advice of a local
expert, my neighbour John Wright, who is a passionate mycologist.
He leads fungus forays in early October and November, from the
Kingcombe Centre in West Dorset.

Nb. Always obey the courtesy of the countryside code, take
care as regards access to land, and remember to pick wisely.

Good hunting!

Fair trade in Dorset

CLIPPER TEAS HAVE achieved much: as the world's first ever Fairtrade tea company they were the first to operate a minimum-pricing policy for tea, and with their minimum three-year trading agreement they put their money where their mouth is as regards commitment to partners and growers overseas, helping to create truly sustainable development – and of course they produce excellent teas. It's obviously a policy that works well for Clipper as they have become a force to be reckoned with. Along the way they've picked up some 14 organic food awards, 15 Great Taste awards and various brand and packaging gongs. With about a third of the organic tea market under their belt Clipper are helping to put Dorset firmly on the map.

It all starts with the tea-plant, *Camellia sinensis*. They use 2 major varieties, the Chinese type which favours cooler mountain slopes, and the Indian, which thrives best in the hotter, steamier atmospheres. Consequently, they have differing characters like the smooth, subtle Darjeeling, from the north, which is my own personal favourite, and the spicier, fuller Assam from the warmer climes. Expert tasters in Clipper's tea laboratory maintain consistency by daily tastings, boiling water poured over leaves and brewed just as we would at home, then slurped over the tastebuds like a wine.

Of course, tea is not actually grown in the county but they do use Dorset applewood to smoke their own distinctive Lapsang Souchong – that relieves me, as I had always assumed lapsang was flavoured with the distilled essence of tarry old railway sleepers!

Here's a novel way of smoking your fish at home using tea.

TEA-SMOKED MACKEREL

Place a large square of foil in a wok (to stop the mix burning onto the metal) and put the tea and sugar on it. (The sugar infuses the smoke with caramel, and helps the flavour penetrate.) Lay another square over the tea leaves and place the bamboo steamer on top. Slice 2 fillets off the bone, removing fins (and scales if mackerel is not used), but leaving the skin on, then season lightly and place in the steamer. Cover with the lid (use foil to seal if no lid) and place over a high flame until the tea begins to smoke, then reduce the flame to very low and smoke the fish for 10–12 minutes or so. Timing will vary according to to the degree of heat and the thickness of the fillets. Serve with rice and your favourite green vegetable.

Serves: 2
Preparation time: 10 minutes
Cooking time: 12 minutes

1 fresh mackerel (perfect to take up smoke flavours but you can use other types of oily fish like salmon or halibut)

2 tbsp white sugar

6 tbsp Lapsang Souchong loose tealeaves (try green tea or a Darjeeling to give a lighter result)

aluminium foil

1 wok (with lid)

1 bamboo Chinese steamer

Maldon salt and freshly ground black pepper

Our orchard heritage

IN 1839 THERE were over 100 acres of orchard in the parish of Symondsbury, and the remains of this natural heritage are still very much alive in the gardens and orchards of Dorset villages and towns. The Symondsbury Apple Project is a community-based voluntary organisation, and is part of 2005's Heritage Orchard Year, supported by the Local Heritage Initiative.

Based in Bridport at the Centre for Local Food they organise educational courses with practical demonstrations: as learning skills from a book is quite difficult, with diagrams sometimes bearing no resemblance to what's actually in front of you, SAP's David Squirrell developed a 1-day course expressly to give people the opportunity to learn how to tackle both young and old trees in need of restoration. One of the Project's main aims is to encourage people to actively maintain our apple heritage and our trees and orchards.

Monique is head chef at Parnham House, my publisher's Dorset residence, and brings her French finesse to bear in her daily cuisine. She uses produce sourced locally, much of it from the gardens at Parnham, and her well-used recipe for a delicious lemony apple tart is much appreciated.

APPLE AND LEMON TART

Measure flour into a large bowl, add fats, mix together until resembling fine breadcrumbs. Add egg yolk, stir until the mixture collects to a dough, adding a little water if necessary. Knead pastry very lightly, then wrap and chill for about 30 minutes. Preheat oven (200°C/gas mark 6). Cut cooking apples into quarters, remove core, chop (unpeeled) apple into chunks.

In a large pan place prepared apples with water. Cover and cook very gently for 10-15 minutes until the apples have become soft and mushy. Rub apple through a medium sieve into a clean pan, add 4 tbsp apricot jam, sugar and lemon zest. Cook on a high heat for 10-15 minutes, stirring constantly, until all excess juices have evaporated and the mixture is thick. Allow to cool.

Roll out the pastry thinly and line a 20cm loose-based fluted flan tin. Bake blind. Spoon the cooled purée into the flan case and level. Peel, quarter and core the eating apples, then slice very thinly. Arrange in neat overlapping circles all over the purée, brush with lemon juice then sprinkle with caster sugar. Return flan to the oven and bake for 25 minutes or until the edges are golden brown.

To glaze, sieve 4 tbsp heated apricot jam then brush all over the top of the fruit and pastry. Serve warm or cold.

Serves: 8
Preparation time: 60 minutes
Cooking time: 45 minutes

Pastry:
180g plain flour
45g unsalted butter, diced
45g vegetable shortening, diced
1 medium egg yolk
cold water, if necessary

Filling:
900g Bramley apples
2 tbsp water
4 tbsp apricot jam
60g caster sugar
grated rind of ½ large lemon
240g eating apples
1-2 tbsp lemon juice
2 tsp caster sugar for sprinkling
4 tbsp apricot jam

Over page: Ewell Fruit Farm

Goats' cheese being made at the
Woolsery Dairy in Up Sydling

Goats' cheese

WOOLSERY DAIRY IS based in Up Sydling near Maiden Newton, where they produce a range of handmade cheeses. The herd of goats is fed as natural a diet as possible. The original goat farm was set up ten years ago producing only milk but about seven years ago they started processing their own milk into a full fat hard cheese which has very good keeping qualities. Since then, other cheeses have been developed: they make several soft cheeses in pots, individual rounds or logs, and some using organic cow's milk from local farms under Soil Association certification. Woolsery English Goats' Cheese has won the coveted British Cheese Awards 'Cheese Lovers Trophy' and other cheeses in the range have won silver and bronze awards.

Here's a goats' cheese dish that has a refined flavour with the benefit of the 'bite' of polenta. Those who say they don't like polenta as it is has no flavour are missing the point. It's like saying potatoes have no flavour. It's all about texture and the ability of the cornmeal to absorb seasonings. I adapted this from a recipe donated by Bruce Jones, a talented Aussie chef and friend who I have worked alongside for over 15 years in the busy milieu of the film industry. We have seen food preferences change over that time to healthier meals and this tart is typical of the lighter cuisine film crews demand nowadays – although it goes without saying a bacon bap will never go out of style!

GOATS' CHEESE, LEEK AND POLENTA TART

Lightly oil the springform tin, lining the sides with baking parchment 1cm proud of the top edge. Cut the red onions into 5mm wedges, place in a roasting tray, sprinkle them with the vinegar, and bake for 30 minutes (200°C/gas mark 6), basting at least once. Meanwhile, bring the milk/water mix to the boil, pour in the polenta, seasoning with a pinch of salt, black pepper and the vegetable stock powder. Simmer for 3 minutes or so, stirring briskly to prevent sticking, until the polenta comes away from the sides of the pan, then remove from heat and stir in 70g butter. Add grated parmesan and fold in. When mixed, it should resemble the consistency of a thick porridge. Spoon into the tin and smooth flat. You should have at least a 2cm layer. Allow to set.

Sauté the leeks in the remaining 20g butter (I usually add a small dash of olive oil to prevent burning) and sweat gently for 10-12 minutes until softened. Layer the onions evenly over the polenta base, then cover with the cooked leeks. Whisk up the eggs and cream, seasoning with salt, white pepper and mace, then pour over the leek topping; break up the goat's cheese with your fingers and spread over the top evenly. Finish with a few grinds of black pepper and bake (200°C/gas mark 6) for about 30–35 minutes or so, until there are brown edges on the goats' cheese and the eggy layer is not runny. Rest for some 15 minutes to ensure the tart is set and can be cut neatly with a razor-sharp knife.

This recipe is to fill a 25cm springform tin and will serve 10
Preparation time: 30 minutes
Cooking time: 50 minutes

2 x 150g Woolsery soft goats' cheese

3 handfuls (about 150g) coarse polenta

4 medium leeks (including green flags only if tender) washed, sliced diagonally not too fine

350ml water/milk mixture (50:50)

90g unsalted butter

Maldon salt and freshly ground black pepper

90g coarsely grated Parmesan cheese

1 heaped tsp vegetarian (Marigold) stock powder

3 medium red onions, peeled

2 tbsp 'syrupy' balsamic vinegar

6 medium eggs

400ml double cream

generous pinch white pepper

generous pinch ground mace

olive oil

'Pumpkins For Sale'

DORSET SOMETIMES YIELDS unexpected rewards. Last October, near Halloween time, I spied a sign indicating 'Pumpkins For Sale' and decided to about-turn and investigate. The track led to a barn belonging to Mr Measures. A small-holder, Mr Measures had turned his hand to many fruit and vegetables in his life and in his youth worked with livestock, particularly sheep. Sadly he suffers from a fair degree of crippling arthritis, the result of over-exposure to organophosphate pesticides in sheep dips, from a time when health standards and awareness were not at the forefront of people's thoughts. But he bears his gnarled hands with an inspiringly cheerful disposition, and he was happy to display the myriad of growing projects in his polytunnels.

It is his squashes that I remember most. An impressively varied display, quite unlike any other I've come across. A family member sent him seeds from New England of the more unusual cultivars. He regales me with tales of agricultural experimentation over the decades and eventually sells me some choice squash for a few pounds. I feel that I got the better deal, as I have just had some 30 minutes entertainment as well as wending my way home with an armful of exotic pumpkins that would put the bland pile at the local Morrisons to shame. I was told later that he would soon be truly retiring, so I felt both uplifted by meeting him and a little sad that it was probably his last crop.

To fill the gap, Bothen Hill Produce is my recommendation for all your pumpkin requirements. In fact, they are a good all-round source of organic vegetable varieties. They even stock the exotic Poblano pepper with its distinctive smoky flavour (see soup recipe below). They sell direct from their base in Bothenhampton, on the road from Bridport to West Bay, and operate a regular box scheme as well as supplying wholesale. Owner Chip de Greeff is happy to advise people as to what is in season. He is rightly proud of his varieties of squash with their differing textures and subtle flavours and offers some simple serving ideas:

WHOLE ROASTED SQUASH

Cut the squash in half and remove the seeds and pith. Drizzle with a peppery olive oil, and if desired, place a clove of crushed garlic in the centre of each half. Roast in a medium oven for approximately 45 minutes or until tender. To serve, scoop out the flesh, or just serve in the skin. 'Uchiki Kuri' is particularly good for this dish, making an excellent starter for at least 4 people.

ROAST VEGETABLE MEDLEY

Squash makes an excellent addition to any roast vegetable dish, as it adds
a wonderful sweetness, but do remember that it doesn't take quite as long
to cook as traditional root vegetables. Cut it up into bite-sized pieces
and add to a dish of any combination of: carrots, parsnips, swede, celeriac,
turnips or scorzonera. Drizzle with a flavoursome olive oil, dot with
butter and garlic, season with Maldon salt and fresh ground black pepper.
For a stronger flavour, sprinkle with some fresh chopped rosemary and/or
thyme. It may well be necessary to delay adding your squash to the other
vegetables; some of the denser varieties take as long to cook but others
need only 30 or 40 minutes. Use your own judgement, bearing in mind
that the odd charred corner is good.

ROASTED SQUASH AND POBLANO SOUP

Peel and de-seed the squash; place in a roasting tin, drizzle with olive
oil and put in a medium oven (180°C/gas mark 4). After approximately
15 minutes add the pepper and onion. Bake for a further 20 minutes or
until tender. Meanwhile prepare 1½ pints of vegetable stock. Remove
the vegetables from the oven, draining off any excess oil, and add to the
stock mixture. Season to taste. Bring to the boil and simmer for 5 minutes.
Check seasoning again. Remove from heat and liquidise. Return
to low heat, add a quarter of a pint of milk and reheat but do not boil.
Add additional liquid if too thick for taste (but this soup is really at its
best with a thick texture).

    Serve piping hot garnished with a little cream and a sprinkle
of parsley with warm organic wholemeal bread on the side.

Serves: 4
Preparation time: 5 minutes
Cooking time: 50 minutes

1 medium organic squash★

50ml good olive oil

1 medium organic red onion,
peeled, finely chopped

½ Poblano pepper,
finely chopped★★

1 large onion, finely chopped

950ml vegetable stock

Maldon sea salt and freshly
ground black pepper

175ml whole milk

★Crown Prince or Butternut
  are best

★★available from Peppers by Post

Pampered Pigs

THE CROCKER FAMILY had been farming in the picturesque village of Tolpuddle for over 100 years until Kevin and Amanda Crocker moved Pampered Pigs Pantry to Rye Hill this year. They have expanded the home farm to create a more interactive environment, so visiting customers and their families can learn about how food is produced, and kids spend time enjoying the animals in a relaxed setting. They will have, in addition to piglets and cows, chickens, goats and lambs, displays of local crafts and photographs, wildlife walks complete with bluebell woods, and ponds with yellow flag irises. They intend to make this not only the centre for their new retail premises but also a destination for all their customers to enjoy. The farm graze a 60-plus herd of cattle at Bere Regis, and they run their famous pigs, and some ewes to provide the new season's lamb from the end of April.

They have recently foregone their organic status. They had to pull out as it was costing too much to produce pork under the various constraints, which meant they couldn't get the returns unless stuff was sold in London, and that meant expending unnecessary 'food miles', defeating the principles of local distribution the Crockers believed in. But they still use the eco-friendly farming methods developed over time. As Kevin is not a fan of the flavour of milk-reared pork, pigs are fed natural vegetables, fodder beet, turnips supplemented by root veg (waste stock from the shop), as well as grain and some GM-free concentrates in the winter season. A little silage helps the roughage quota.

The pigs also like the potato-flake compressed 'trays' sourced from organic distributors, which they enjoy playing with and then eating. So, how do you actually pamper your pigs? EC regulations say pigs must be provided with toys – but the Crockers' pigs have always had footballs and tyres to play with. Kevin assures people that he also talks to them nicely – most of the time.

The Crockers believe strongly in rearing happy animals naturally for local sale, and provenance is not just a buzzword but has an important farming philosophy behind it. Accordingly, the shop sources as much produce locally as it can and it is heart-warming to see traditional country foodstuffs like venison, faggots, boiling fowl and wild rabbits available as well as their excellent range of organic grocery, gourmet pork sausages, gammons and bacon. You can order a whole hog for spit-roasting for a special occasion: it can feed at least 150 guests.

Dorset pork is delicious as a traditional roast, but here's a recipe that really hits the tastebuds. It was donated by a chef chum, Alan Coxon, whose name you may recognise from his series on *BBC 2*, or from *UK Food*. He is a very knowledgeable chap about food and food history. The Burmese style here incorporates a little *nam pla* (fish sauce), lime and brown sugar to add that sweet-and-sour effect, with small Thai peppers being recommended for this dish. Alan's general rule of thumb is that the smaller the chilli, the hotter the flavour.

BURMESE-STYLE PORK CURRY

With the exception of the water or stock, soy sauce, *nam pla* or lime juice, mix meat together with all ingredients in a large bowl. In a heavy based pan, heat oil (you may need to brown the meat in 4 or so batches, so 1 tbsp oil at a time will be sufficient) and add a layer of pork. Stir thoroughly, turn down the heat, cooking until the meat has changed colour and the curry is fragrant. Put aside. Repeat with the rest of the meat. Add liquids to all the pork and bring to the simmer, stirring occasionally. Cook for 18-20 minutes or until pork is tender.

Serve with Thai jasmine rice or:

CUMIN-SCENTED SWEET POTATOES

Peel sweet potatoes (allow up to 250g unpeeled weight per person) and cut into large chunks. Bring a large pan of salted water to the boil with 2 tbsp cumin seeds and boil/simmer the sweet potato until about 90% cooked through, then drain, and while still hot add a medium tin of full-fat coconut milk and stir the potatoes around until cooked right through. This will take another 2-3 minutes or so, but don't overcook or they'll get mushy. The coconut will thicken to a creamy coating. Throw in a handful of chopped fresh coriander leaves, turn through. Serve hot.

Serves: 4
Preparation time: 30 minutes
Cooking time: 20 minutes

675g diced pork loin chunks (3cm square)★

2½cm piece fresh root ginger, peeled, grated

6 fresh chillies, finely sliced (reduce the amount to 3 for a milder version)

2 tbsp dark brown sugar (ideally palm sugar, or jaggery)

2 tsp ground turmeric

1 tbsp Thai red curry paste

4 shallots, finely chopped

3 cloves garlic, crushed

600ml water or chicken stock

1 tsp soy sauce

3 tbsp tamarind liquid (or juice and zest of 1 extra lime)

1 tbsp *nam pla* (fish sauce)

zest and juice 1 lime

4 tbsp oil

★I have used pork boneless spare rib steaks (from below the shoulder) as a cheaper alternative to good effect

Cheddar-making at Denhay

DENHAY FARMS IS an award-winning business, 3 miles inland as the crow flies from the Jurassic Coast World Heritage Site, in Dorset's Marshwood Vale. For two generations their traditional approach to cheese production methods and high standards have kept them at the top and in 2002 earned them the Royal Agricultural Society of England Award for Excellence in Practical Farming.

George Streatfeild, the current Managing Director, is rightly proud of their PDO accreditation, that is, Protected Designation of Origin, an acknowledgement of Denhay's cheddar being made using authenticated methods and local milk. PDO status is the equivalent to *Appellation Controlée* for French wine.

Over the years Denhay has expanded to 1900 acres, with 950 Friesian Holstein cows in 5 herds, selected for the high protein quality of their milk. They are fed grass and/or maize silage, supplemented with cereals – mainly wheat and soya. All the milk produced is made into Traditional Farmhouse Cheddar. September–October cheese is best, made with milk from freshly-calved cows.

Turning cheeses on the maturing racks several times a week, and then later a few times a month, is crucial to allow correct moisture control and hence development of flavours. By about 9 months the cheeses are mature, and after 12 months the full-flavoured cheese is perfect in George's opinion for a grilled cheese-on-toast treat. He swears that you can't beat it, especially with a slice of tomato on top!

Portland and its sheep

DIANA AND BOB Clarke of Meerhay Manor inhabit a picturesque area of Beaminster that features a quite unique farming story. They breed Portland sheep, a heathland breed belonging to the Wessex tan-faced group. This handsome breed originally grazed on the windblown promontory that is Portland, a rather bleak, treeless, rocky outcrop to the south of Weymouth at the end of the 18-mile long Chesil bank; they are the only native sheep hardy enough to graze here, given the limited amount of topsoil.

The history of the Portlands is rather patchy, not surprising as shepherds don't usually record their experiences on paper, and information has usually to be gleaned from interested observers and agricultural historians. Originally kept to trade wool and pay tithes in ewe's milk cheese, in time the meat gained a reputation for excellence. Indeed, a report in 1812 by William Stevenson records over 3000 sheep on the island and 'It is said to be as fine a flavoured mutton as any in the kingdom'. King George III himself, on his visits to Weymouth, always demanded Portland mutton, as did the Queen's Own Yeomanry during their annual dinner at The Gloucester Hotel. Despite such widespread popularity, the premium price demanded for the meat from such small carcasses made the breed uneconomic. Various cross-breeding was tried but most did not survive the harsh conditions. Quarrying the famous Portland Stone contributed to their decline until the last Portlands left in 1920.

The southernmost tip of Dorset plays host to the hardiest of sheep

By 1973 only 79 breeding ewes were left in the country as a whole. At that stage, the Rare Breed Survival Trust was created and thanks to a band of dedicated activists the island was restocked in 1977 by the Portland Field Research Group, in some part helped by the locals. The prison briefly took over the husbandry to aid inmates' rehabilitation and to supply the prison farm. Sadly, the breed was again lost to the island after government budget cuts dictated cessation of on-site prison farm projects. For those interested in finding out more, I can highly recommend the 2003 publication by Norman Jones, a retired naval Officer, of *Portland Sheep – A Breed With History*.

Latterly Diana and Bob have been successful enough with their own small flock to have reintroduced this valuable breed back to its rightful home. They are valuable for many reasons: the fleece is much prized by hand spinners, the meat is excellent, and they are easy to keep. They are also unusual in not having docked tails, and in both rams and ewes the horns describe a dramatic and heavily-spiralled shape.

Portland lamb is regarded as tasting quite different from other breeds, and to put that reputation to the test the Clarkes conjured a superb lunch with a slow-roasted shoulder that emerged from the Aga in a steamy cloud of tantalising meaty scent. All of which, I hasten to add, was demolished by the lunch guests with a pile of mashed potatoes to mop up the juices. The verdict? Excellent – strong-tasting melt-in-the-mouth flesh without being too gamy. Diana has kindly presented us with the method so you can enjoy the Portland experience yourselves.

SLOW-ROASTED SHOULDER OF PORTLAND LAMB

Put the joint in a stout cast iron or earthenware pot and cover with the beans and their liquid, the wine, onions and shallots. Scatter over the bay and rosemary, purée, garlic, tomatoes, some crushed black peppercorns and a generous sprinkling of salt. If you are using an Aga then cover the casserole and place it in the simmering oven for 4 hours and then transfer to the hotter roasting oven for another hour. If an ordinary cooker is used, then roast at 150°C/gas mark 2 for 4 hours and then turn up the thermostat to 220°C/gas mark 7 for the last hour. Do have a look at it now and then and give it a prod and stir. At the end of cooking time, the flesh will fall off the bone and all the shoulder's fat will have melted into the vegetables.

Serve in deep dinner soup plates with whatever takes your fancy. A green salad and crusty bread is great but I recommend the Clarkes' simple addition of mashed potatoes with spring onions to mop up the gravy.

Serves: 8
Preparation time: 5 minutes
Cooking time: 5 hours

1 large shoulder of lamb
(ask your butcher to cut off the knuckle end, but keep it to enrich the casserole)

2 large tins haricot beans, juices reserved

450ml medium white wine

2 large onions, sliced coarse

10 shallots, quartered

6 large tomatoes, quartered

3 tbsp tomato purée

10 whole cloves of garlic, peeled

3 large sprigs of fresh rosemary

3 bay leaves

Maldon sea salt and freshly crushed black peppercorns

MANY AUTUMNAL RECIPES benefit from the richness of a home-made stock, well reduced. I give recipes here because you cannot intensify the flavour of a shop-bought stock: reducing it would give an unacceptably salty result.

VEAL STOCK

Brown veal and beef bones/trimmings in a hot oven (220°C/gas mark 7) for 15-20 minutes then place in a large, preferably tall, stockpot with all ingredients then boil, skim and simmer for 4 hours. Strain through a fine sieve lined with muslin, and reduce over a high heat by at least half to render it strong tasting. You should end up with about 0.75 litre of a well-flavoured liquid (just over 1 pint or so). Rest liquid in the fridge for a couple of hours to ensure fat residue can be removed easily after it cools.

CHICKEN STOCK

Make as per veal recipe above substituting chicken bones for veal/beef, – but add 1 leek, chopped; omit tomato purée; and adding some extra chicken wings will intensify the flavour. If your chicken was supplied with giblets you can add these, but bear in mind the stock will be heavier.

Cooking time: 5 hours

1kg veal bones and trimmings

450g beef bones and trimmings (both chopped short to fit pan)

60g streaky bacon

1 tsp tomato purée

60g each finely chopped carrots, mushrooms, onions, leeks

1 large fresh tomato, de-seeded/skinned

1 shallot, peeled and chopped

1 garlic clove, peeled and crushed

300ml white wine

1 litre cold water

bunch parsley stalks

pinch of dried tarragon, chervil

bouquet garni (thyme, parsley, bay)

3 black peppercorns

1 clove

Portland Ram at Shedbush Farm

Winter

The Cobb, Lyme Regis
22 February 2005, 12.40pm

Bakery traditions

WHEN I FIRST moved to Maiden Newton in 2003, I was made aware of Norman House when locals nervously whispered in hushed tones that they were afraid he might retire – 'how will we manage?' Who was this pillar of society, I wondered? Did he own the county? Had he been delivering generations of babies? Not quite… but his bread was the stuff of life in the village. Norman chuckled a bit when I told him this and said, with some degree of flour on his hands, that he'd been technically retired for over a year. (You could have fooled me.) On a tour of the W E House bakery, which had an original solid Victorian iron oven, everything had an air of continuity and tradition. His father took it over in the 1890s, and Norman still used traditional skills and proving methods to bake white, wholemeal and multigrain breads. Norman's brown loaf is legendary and he is keen to point out the importance of the protein content. But time marches on and since that meeting with Norman, he retired in earnest in the spring of 2005, though his son Graham went on bread-making for the new owner, Sarah Woolcott during the changeover period. The business is known as 'The Bakery'. Graham used to ensure the other grocery lines, like honey, hams and other delicacies were up to standard, with a nice little sideline in ales from respected breweries. Let's hope that's another tradition that continues. Norman and Graham also always kept their back-door customers happy with their bread… fat trout in the river and greedy little ducklings that all literally jumped for the chance to chew on a bit of history. Now it's your turn. I have managed to twist his arm and get his simple apple cake recipe on record: Norman's legacy to us all.

NORMAN'S DORSET APPLE CAKE

Mix the flour, baking powder and salt together in a large mixing bowl. Dice the fat into small pieces and mix in evenly. Add the egg/milk liquid and whisk together until smooth, then fold in the apple until evenly mixed. Grease a rectangular baking tray with butter (you can use baking parchment) and flour well, then spread the cake mix level with a spatula and bake for 30–35 minutes (approx) at 200°C/gas mark 6 until the mix has risen and set.

Cool on a wire rack, sprinkle with castor sugar, then cut into fingers for serving. This is best eaten fresh as the moisture in the fruit will leak out and make it soggy over time, which doesn't spoil the taste but which loses the contrast between cakey sponge and chunky fruit.

Serves: 8
Preparation time: 15 minutes
Cooking time: 35 minutes

360g plain flour

8g baking powder

pinch salt

170g margarine★

170g castor sugar

2 medium eggs, mixed with:

285ml milk

720g Bramley cooking apples, cut into 1cm cubes★★

★You can use butter, but it will give a somewhat crisper texture. Norman says you can use a 50:50 mix with margarine if preferred

★★This is gross weight before peeling and coring. Some people also use raisins. Not here

A Dorset giant

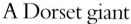

PERCY FUDGE FOUNDED the eponymous bakery in 1926, going door-to-door delivering produce made from local ingredients. He won awards and was a great innovator. However by the Sixties, the decade of Mother's Pride and Wonderloaf, times were tough due to competitive pricing by the big conglomerates, and Fudges survived by expanding the cake and pastries side and catering for parties and weddings. Percy's son Dennis supplied the hotel trade in the seventies, and in the eighties helped define a new future for the bakery with Steve Graham, granddaughter Sue's husband. Steve had studied continental traditions and methods in Düsseldorf, and developed new ranges defined by great taste, good shelf life and quality ingredients. Fudges allied themselves with top Dorset suppliers like Denhay cheese and Blackmore Vale cream, and started new lines like moulded shortbread. Now Fudges have an industrial-sized factory, and yet still continue to bake stunning products. They make top-quality traditional and modern items (some for bespoke retail outlets like Fortnum & Mason).

Sue underlines the Fudges philosophy, so near to mine: good ingredients; resist the low-fat low-salt *ersatz* efforts of the mass-multiples; and keep traditional recipes. Low-fat diets and GI and Atkins may come and go but quality will survive; I've never seen the point of a diet-doughnut and Sue concurs. You just have to taste Fudges savoury range of flatbreads and my sweet favourite, florentines, to understand the love that created them.

Proud to be organic

TAMARISK FARM IS one of the oldest established family organic farms in Dorset, proudly stating their Soil Association Certification number as 07. Josephine Pearse and her husband Arthur are the elder statesmen of the family, with Adam and Ellen Simon following in their footsteps. They raise beef cattle and sheep, as well as growing arable and vegetable crops, especially salads. Arthur is particularly keen on new varieties: Japanese chrysanthemums, mizuna, the ever popular pak-choi and the newer shungiku or 'chop-suey' greens all flourish. As you would expect, holistic methods are the norm and Ellen is keen on letting soil rest, using green manures such as red clovers and other legumes to fix nitrogen naturally in the soil, and lucerne to allow and encourage the uptake of important minerals through the deep tap-root system. Adam is strongly in favour of the use of natural manures, warning that industrial fertilisers work for a few years but then the soil lacks organic matter: you need to feed the soil not the plant. Tamarisk also seeds 'beetle-banks' at the side of fields to ensure the eco-system (the myriad of tiny insects, worms and wildlife) is maintained.

Another producer of fine beef, mutton and lamb is Peter Broatch of Eweleaze Farm, near Osmington, where he has farmed for over 5 years. Eweleaze has steeply sloping land, and is cursed with a heavy clay soil, great for mineral content but slippery and boggy in wet weather. He farms Aberdeen Angus cattle and tries to get them to a maturity that is only capped by government regulation, brought in after the BSE crisis, although Peter proclaims that there has never been a case of BSE on an organically-run farm. Feedstuffs are scrutinised for full-organic quality and as Peter likes his cattle to have a varied diet, they are often grazed at Radipole on marshy land, feeding on reeds and other marshy greenery. His sheep are a mixture of Dorset Down and Poll Dorsets, some crossed with a Soay ram (originally a St. Kilda variety) that makes them hardier. Peter believes it is important that animals not only have a stress-free life, but stay calm before slaughtering. Stress causes chemical changes within the animal flesh that toughens it so before the meat is processed and hung (3-4 weeks minimum for beef, lamb for 7-10 days) Peter prefers to keep his stock's journey to the slaughterhouse as short as possible.

Peter's pride: his Angus herd

Peter keeps up to 1,000 hens for egg production, using the slowest growing of the commercial breeds – the Hubbard 257 – which he experimented with for meat production before deciding to make eggs the mainstay of the business. He actually thinks highly enough of his birds to eat the old boilers himself – the breasts are OK for roasting he assures me, and the rest fine for a casserole.

He has been building his own house, and long-term plans are to expand locally and encourage young people to appreciate at grass roots level what constitutes good food. I admire his resolve and his appreciation of the importance of the link between suppliers and consumers – and his support of Farmers' Markets and that connection. As he says 'Farming is a very sobering profession, accepting yourself as a part of nature – you have to work with nature'.

The components of this dish can all be made in advance so it makes a great dinner party starter. Peter Broatch of Eweleaze Farm kindly lent this popular recipe from one of the restaurants he supplies, the excellent Sienna in the high street in Dorchester, to whom I am indebted.

CELERIAC SOUP WITH BRAISED BEEF TORTELLINI

Start by braising the beef for the tortellini filling. Slice the vegetables and lay in a small roasting tin. Trim the shin of excess fat, slice into 2cm thick pieces, season and dust with flour. Seal meat in small batches in hot oil, colouring well. Lay the meat on top of the vegetables, scatter thyme and bay leaf over, then lay pancetta (or bacon) slices on top. Pour in the wine and stock. Simmer, then cover with foil and braise in an oven (150°C/gas mark 2-3). Times vary; start checking after 1 hour and then every 15-20 minutes until cooked. Meat should be very tender.

Remove meat from the tin, when cool, shred finely with two forks. Pass the braising liquid through a fine sieve, pressing well on the vegetables to extract as much liquid as possible. Reduce braising liquid to about 100ml, skimming any foam off the surface. Add half the reduced braising liquid to the meat (reserving the remainder) and mix in well. Taste, adjust seasoning. Refrigerate tortellini filling until needed.

To make the soup, peel and dice onion, slice the leek (1cm pieces), washing well. Peel celeriac and cut into (1cm) cubes. Sweat vegetables in oil until soft. Add stock and simmer until vegetables are tender. Allow to cool, then liquidise soup, passing through a fine sieve into a clean pan. Add cream then season to taste (thin with a little more vegetable stock if necessary). The soup should be silky and the consistency of thick double cream.

Serves: 6
Preparation time: 1½ hours
Cooking time: 2 hours

Soup:
1 small onion
1 small leek
1 small celeriac
1 litre vegetable stock
100ml double cream
salt and pepper
50ml olive oil

Pasta dough:
1 whole egg plus yolks
to make total weight of 120g
200g pasta flour
10g olive oil
½ tsp salt

Beef filling:
500g beef shin
1 stick celery
1 small onion
1 small leek
1 small carrot
1 bay leaf
1 small bunch thyme
4 slices pancetta/smoked
streaky bacon
200ml beef stock
400ml red wine
flour for dusting
olive oil for frying

For the pasta, weigh pasta flour into a food processor bowl. Weigh eggs, oil and salt into a jug and whisk together. Start the processor and add egg mixture through the feed tube. Process until a breadcrumb texture is achieved. Tip the pasta mix onto a clean work-surface and knead well for a few minutes. Form into a thick roll, lightly coat with olive oil and wrap in cling film. Refrigerate for 30 minutes. To form tortellini, divide pasta into three and roll out on a pasta machine to thickness no. 6. Cut out circles using a 75mm pastry cutter. Repeat with the remaining dough to give 18 circles then cover them with a just-damp tea towel. Working with 2 or 3 circles at a time, place teaspoonfuls of beef mixture in the centres of the circles. Brush edges lightly with water and form into half-moon parcels. Crimp edges together well, and then bring the ends around and squeeze together to form a classic tortellini shape. Squeeze the joints well so that the pasta is not too thick. Repeat with remaining pasta circles, and place finished tortellini on a floured surface. (Any remaining pasta or beef can be frozen). If using straight away, cook the tortellini in simmering salted water for 4 minutes. If for use later (up to 24 hours), blanch in simmering water for 30 seconds, refresh in iced water, drain and toss in a little olive oil. Refrigerate until needed and then cook as above.

To serve, reheat the soup, cook the tortellini and place in the centre of shallow bowls. Pour the soup around. Reheat the remaining braising liquid and drizzle through the soup.

River Cottage

I HAVE FOLLOWED Hugh Fearnley-Whittingstall's efforts from the early days of *A Cook On The Wild Side* through the riveting *River Cottage* series. Hugh has a fundamental appreciation of what constitutes good eating, and an undeniable passion for ingredients of quality, tending to the 'less is more' principle: if a foodstuff is grown or reared carefully, and is cooked gracefully, it should be allowed to speak for itself in the democratic forum of the kitchen cauldron.

River Cottage HQ is somewhat unique in that it is not a restaurant (they can't take bookings for lunch or dinner), a cooking school, or purely for food demonstrations: it's a food masterclass. I squeezed in at the end of one of the long tables at an interactive dinner, questions invited. The evening teetered on the edge of a party, the glue binding everyone there, dedicated foodies or not, being the love of the country and its produce.

This recipe comes from *Meat*. Hugh loves this because

It's so fantastically forgiving – the rich seams of fat keep the meat tender and juicy, no matter how long you cook it for. I tend to concentrate on getting the crackling right and the rest just falls into place. The citrus juice and zest keep the sauce aromatic as well as tart.

ROAST BELLY OF PORK WITH APPLE SAUCE
Score the skin of the belly with a sharp knife (a Stanley knife is surprisingly handy) and rub with salt, pepper and fresh thyme leaves getting the seasoning and herbs right into the cracks. Roast in a hot oven (220°C/gas mark 7) for 30 minutes, then turn down the oven to 180°C/gas mark 4 and cook for roughly another hour, until the juices run clear when the meat is pierced with a skewer and the crackling has crackled to an irresistible golden brown. If the crackling is reluctant, whack up the heat again as high as you like and check every few minutes until it's done.

To make the sauce, peel, core and slice the Bramleys, tossing them with the lemon juice as you go. Put them in a pan with the orange zest and juice and a first sprinkling of sugar. Cook gently until the apples break up into a rough puree, then check for sweetness and adjust to your taste. Keep warm (or re-heat gently to serve).

Remove the crackling from the pork before carving, then cut the joint into thick slices. Serve each person one or two slices with a good piece of crackling and bring the apple sauce to the table. I like to serve this with mashed potatoes not roast as there's already plenty of fat and crispness on the plate. Some simple lightly steamed greens such as Savoy cabbage, spinach or curly kale will help to ease your conscience as you lap up the lard.

Serves: about 8
Preparation time: 5 minutes
Cooking time: 1 hour 35 minutes

the thick end of the belly (last 6 ribs)

fresh thyme leaves

salt and freshly ground black pepper

Apple sauce:

3-4 large Bramley apples

a squeeze of lemon juice

grated zest (no pith) and juice of ½ orange

1-2 tbsp caster sugar (to taste)

Cheese…

MICHAEL DAVIES IS the epitome of the gentleman farmer. An ex-naval officer's son, he has farmed at Woodbridge Farm at Sturminster Newton for over 30 years. He trained at Cannington in Somerset as a cheesemaker, milking by hand, and then went on to build up a farm of over 600 acres. The introduction of milk quotas shook things up and he had to figure out how to diversify from solely dairy farming. Blue cheese was an obvious choice as Blue Vinney had been made in Dorset for some time with varying degrees of success. Mike decided it was time to put it on the map. He has striven to improve and uphold the quality of this high-profile Dorset cheese, made to this day with hand-skimmed unpasteurised milk, and thus subject to frequent Environmental Health inspections. He has obtained a PGI label for his dairy (a protected geographic indicator), a benchmark for designating and protecting the geographic origins of his product, of which he is rightly proud. Mike prefers the milk from a winter yield, slightly more acidic due to the silage and maize supplements fed at that season, with more body. Milk batches of 1600 litres every day go to make about 28 cheeses and it takes 12-16 weeks for the blue mould (nowadays inoculated from a consistent spore culture) to develop and mature the cheeses. It is a light, slightly crumbly blue cheese, more like a Cheshire than a Stilton. Any problems I enquire? Not at this end he assures me – if only the British consumer were better at keeping cheese.

There is a follow-on success story to the dairy. His daughter Emily started in the trade helping out at shows and markets, and wondered what to do with the bits of cheese left at the end of the day. She experimented with soups and cooked up an award-winning mushroom and bacon soup (with Blue Vinney, naturally). Emily has made soups for Hugh Fearnley-Whittingstall, and made a great commercial success of the Dorset Blue Soup Company.

DORSET KNOBS

Samuel Moores and his wife Eleanor began making Dorset Knobs about one hundred and thirty years ago at Stoke Mills in the Marshwood Vale. Local farm workers traditionally started the day with tea and a knob biscuit. More like a rusk, made of white flour and baked in the faggot-heated oven after the bread, and then again for crunchy texture, it was a favourite of Thomas Hardy's for an impromptu late supper, accompanied by Dorset Blue Vinney.

…and Pickles

——

Whilst flying the flag for small independent producers of gourmet foods I could not help but notice the wealth of jams, chutneys and sauces that abound in our county. Those produced by dedicated individuals (the WI comes to mind) set the bar very high for others trying for a more mechanised production. Forest Products have had a foot in both worlds, having started as a small family firm of jam makers in 1986, and now showing that industrial efficiency doesn't have to compromise standards.

The company recently won Golds at the 2005 Great Taste Awards (they have received a myriad of accolades over the past few years). Forest Products use the best ingredients they can source, in season wherever possible, and run production in relatively small batches, testing sugar levels during and after cooking, which keeps everything on-track. Result? Great taste, consistently. The real ale chutney uses top beers from Badger and Hall & Woodhouse breweries and it actually improves with age in the jar as the flavours mingle. Sadly this year the jam and chutney production has had to move over the county border due to residential opposition to the exhaust from the factory, but thankfully production of Jack and Ollies' Crisps doesn't offend local sensibilities so much and this remains in the area.

Forest Products recipes are closely guarded industrial secrets so instead, I have attempted to give my version of an old eastern-European pickled beetroot recipe, popular in Jewish cuisine, updated and jazzed up with balsamic and a little orange peel and aromatic spice.

CHRAIN (BEETROOT AND HORSERADISH CHUTNEY)

Bring all ingredients to the boil, stirring occasionally to soften and dissolve the sugar. Simmer for 40 minutes and check liquid level. The preserve should be moist but not watery. Spoon the hot chutney into sterilised jars and seal with parchment discs. Especially good with smoked fish.

Preparation time: 10 minutes
Cooking time: 45 minutes

750g beetroot, peeled, coarsely grated

1 medium red onion, finely chopped

450ml balsamic vinegar

230ml water

180g caster sugar

3 tsp yellow grainy mustard

2 cloves

5cm piece of peeled orange rind

10cm piece fresh horseradish root, finely grated

salt and cracked black pepper

THIS DISH ORIGINATED in Spain, where it is called *dulce de membrillo*. It is not a dessert per se, but rather a preserve to go with good cheeses. To turn it into a substantial end to a meal, simply place a couple of slices of Blue Vinney on some fresh halved and peeled pears and grill until the cheese is slightly melted. Serve accompanied by some freshly shelled walnuts with a couple of spoonfuls of strong honey, and a slab of the *membrillo*.

Preparation time: 20 minutes
Cooking time: 40 minutes

1½kg fresh ripe quince

250ml water

450g caster sugar

QUINCE CHEESE

Peel and quarter the quinces, taking care to remove all the hard seed casing in the middle. Chop fruit roughly and put in a preserving pan (or the largest saucepan you have) with the water. Simmer until tender and broken up, then push through a coarse sieve or *mouli* to create a rough purée. Now add the sugar and gently stir and simmer the mixture for about 40 minutes until the mixture is quite thick: it should come away from the sides of the pan like a choux paste.

With a spatula, transfer the paste to a mould about 4cm deep, smooth the surface, and cover. Leave to rest for 2 hours at room temperature. When it's firm, turn onto greaseproof paper. It should keep for a month, wrapped in foil in the fridge.

THIS RECIPE FOR a different style of preserving fruit was given to me by one of my dearest fellow cooks, Michele Gould, who now lives in Holland. It comes from Blok's, her favourite restaurant in Amersfoort. Marco Blok serves it on a spoon with his cheese platter, rather like we would a chutney. I particularly liked it because the fruit is cooked longer than a jam or jelly or even a fruit cheese. Spread on bread or toast it makes a treacly and memorable snack. Apples or a blend of pear and apple can be used to vary the *stroop*.

Preparation time: 10 minutes
Cooking time: 55 minutes

1kg ripe pears

250g soft brown sugar (muscovado)

1 clove

1 cinnamon stick

1 bay leaf

1 star anise

2 tbsp Calvados

PERENSTROOP

Peel and core pears and cut into four. Place all the ingredients in a large pan and cook them on a medium heat, stirring continually, until all the moisture has evaporated (check closely after 40 minutes). The mix should be quite thick. Remove spices and bay leaf and whiz the rest in a blender. Pass the pear pulp through a fine sieve with the help of the back of a spoon and let the pear *stroop* set in the fridge. The *stroop* has a sticky, Marmite-like consistency, and is easier to decant from a shallow jar.

From grain to table

STOATE'S MILL IS a water-driven mill in the north-east corner of Dorset owned by Michael, the fifth generation of Stoates to run the business. Milling in the west country since the middle of last century, from 1947 they have been grinding 3 main types of flour: biscuit (for cakes etc.), bread (strong or gluten-rich grains) and pasta (hard or 'Durum' wheat). Since the wholefood revolution of the late Sixties and Seventies wholemeal flours have been in demand, and with help from the eastern European tradition we have revived the art of sourdough bread making. Most of the speciality grains like rye and spelt come from Hungary, then ground here. Spelt is firmly on the ascent in popularity. Spelt, in case you didn't know, is an old variety of wheat that had been grown without selective breeding, having a naturally smaller ear and a hardened husk that needs rubbing off before being suitable for baking. Spelt is similar to the kind of wheat the ancient Romans would have had and is more digestible for those who are gluten intolerant. Stoate's supply to retail outlets and speciality food manufacturers throughout Dorset and the South West, but not, Michael stresses, to supermarkets. Awards abound and he is most proud of the Soil Association's Organic Food Award.

Alongside Stoate's Mill, Paul Merry runs his bakery school, Panary. A kindred spirit to Michael, he hates mass-produced, processed bread and tries to reinstate the flavours and textures paramount in artisan baking. He also helped to design and develop the wood-fired oven at Long Crichel Bakery for Jamie Campbell.

GUINNESS AND TREACLE BREAD

Paul Hollywood is a chum, a professional chef, who has kindly donated this recipe. He also has his own school, The Bread Academy.

Crush together all the ingredients till well mixed, tip the dough onto a table and knead for 5 minutes. Place the dough into a bowl to rest for 1 hour. Tip out again and shape into a ball, then flatten and roll it up into a round or an oval, place the dough onto a lined baking tray and leave to rise again for 1 hour. Cut several slashes across the bread and dust with wholemeal flour, bake at 200°C/gas mark 6 for 30 minutes, then cool on a wire rack.

Preparation time: ½ hour
Cooking time: ½ hour

350g wholemeal flour

150g plain white flour

8g salt

30g fresh yeast

60ml black treacle

150ml Guinness

130ml water

Savouries, spelt and cobber

BRIDPORT IS VERY lucky to have a choice of bakeries. In the high street there is the wide range of Hussey's bakery products complete with tea-shop (fondly nicknamed the 'oestrogen lounge') where you can sample a wide range of cakes and savouries with the charming ladies of the blue-rinse brigade. Further up on East Street under the landmark green canopy is Leakers. Proprietors Caroline and Paul Parkins have a tiny shop front behind which worked the master baker Aidan Chapman. Leakers was already popular when Aidan joined the staff after a brief Dorset holiday with his wife and two children. They fell in love with the area and Aidan saw an opportunity to expand the bakery's range. He brought his considerable skills and experience to bear and soon his sourdoughs, speciality breads and savouries turned Leakers into a destination point.

Aidan believes knowledge is there to be shared and the new range includes spelt loaves, rye, cider and cheese breads and a whole range of sweet biscuits (my favourite's the pecan flapjack) and savouries. You must try his floored cobber (wholemeal multigrain brown loaves that have been baked on the bare floor of the hot oven) and crunchy date loaf – but you'll soon find a favourite of your own. Aidan uses long fermentations to develop the flavours and textures and strives to get as much water as possible to be absorbed into the dough mix, which increases the shelf life. He believes that we have overdosed a bit in the last 20 years on so much wheat (which may be partly the reason for intolerance), so he provides a wide variety of grains to feast on. There has been a quiet revolution in the understanding of our staple diet and nowadays people will spend the extra cash on his quality loaves, knowing they will get not only the fantastic taste but improved shelf life. As for the future, Aidan has trained up a couple of Polish bakers – already steeped in the eastern-European traditions of sourdoughs – to succeed him. Meanwhile Aidan has moved out and taken over The Town Mill Bakery in Lyme Regis, where he is installing a wood-fired oven.

Thanks to Caroline Parkins for this recipe: perfect for lunch if you don't want a pasty. As a keen meat-eater I think a vegetarian dish really has to have impact to pass muster – this one does.

DELHI DELIGHT

Fry the onions, garlic and ginger in some of the oil over a medium hot flame until softened. Add courgettes, mushrooms and red pepper and cook on until the mushrooms release their juices, and then add drained chickpeas. Mix the curry paste, tomato and yoghurt together, add to vegetables and bubble filling for around 5 more minutes. Season to taste and allow to cool.

For dough mix together the flour, oil and salt and crumble the yeast into a few tablespoons of tepid water. Knead into flour mixture and add dashes of water until dough comes away cleanly from the sides of the bowl. Continue to knead on a floured board until smooth. Divide into 4 and roll each bit into a circle. Spoon the cooled curry into the centre and catch up the edges of the dough using a wet fingertip to seal the edges. Put each into an oiled pudding bowl with the sealed edges at the top and leave to prove in a warm place for at least 15 minutes. Then bake in a hot oven (200°C/gas mark 6) and check after 10-15 minutes. If liked, chopped coriander leaf can be used to enhance the dough mix.

Serves: 4
Preparation time: 20 minutes
Cooking time: ½ hour

Dough:

450g good quality strong white flour

50ml vegetable oil

10g fresh yeast

pinch salt

tepid water

Filling:

3 onions, thinly sliced

4 tbsp vegetable oil

6cm piece of root ginger, peeled, finely chopped

3 cloves garlic, finely chopped

3 ripe courgettes, sliced

240g peeled, chopped mushrooms

2 red peppers, cored, thinly sliced

800g tin of prepared chickpeas, drained

½ tin chopped tomatoes

4 tbsp natural yoghurt

curry paste to taste

salt and freshly milled black pepper

Wild pigs

Serves: 3-4
Preparation time: 20 minutes
Cooking time: 1 hour
10 minutes

1kg wild boar, boned and rolled leg joint

2 shallots, finely diced

1 tbsp olive oil

finely grated zest of 1 lemon

100g semi-dried cherries

fresh ground black pepper

sprig of fresh rosemary

250ml red wine

2 tsp redcurrant jelly

1 tsp good balsamic vinegar

THERE WAS SOME panic in the local press in 2004 about rebels from a herd of wild boar near Waytown that escaped and started to terrorise local farmers' wives hanging out their washing. Some were recovered but a few hung about and aggressively defended their territory. But then like all such local news it faded and I often wondered what happened to them. It turns out they ended up at Barrow Boar, just over the Somerset border, where Alan Wood has a substantial exotic meat business that also sells buffalo, ostrich and kid. The native variety of boar he keeps is basically a strain of pig that endured before modern breeding diluted the wild pig characteristics, surviving being hunted in the wild, and escaping cross-breeding. As a result, his boars are very hairy and have basically not changed in appearance since the Middle Ages. Taste-wise they are gamier than more domesticated breeds, but can be cooked like ordinary pork although they have no crackling due to the extremely leathery hide. The back fat layer is substantially thicker too. But hams, sausages and all the other piggy pleasures can be created in exactly the same way.

Had Alan noticed any change or trends in eating habits? He was surprised to admit that demand for kid, young goat meat, had skyrocketed – it was always a meat that sold slowly but steadily. Now you can try it – although the herd is grazed just over the county border, Dorset folk can find it at Beaminster Farmers' Market.

Thanks to the Woods for this recipe.

ROAST BOAR WITH A SWEET AND SOUR CHERRY SAUCE

Pre-heat oven to 170°C/gas mark 3. Heat the olive oil in a frying pan and soften shallots slowly without browning. Remove to roasting tin. Increase heat and seal the boar joint on all sides, turning over every few minutes. Remove meat to roasting pan and add zest, black pepper, rosemary and dried cherries. Deglaze the frying pan with some of the red wine, taking care to scrape up any meaty sediment and pour over the meat and cover with foil. Roast for 50-60 minutes until juices run clear.

Lift out meat onto a warm plate along with cherries to rest for at least 10 minutes, add remaining red wine, redcurrant jelly and balsamic to roasting tin, bring to the boil stirring to dissolve jelly. Simmer for a couple of minutes and check seasoning, then strain into a jug, adding juices from the resting meat. Carve and serve as per a regular pork joint with your seasonal accompaniments of choice.

Free-ranging nature
——

BECKLANDS FARM LIES in meadows towards the west of Whitchurch Canonicorum, the home of dedicated organic farmers, Hilary and Francis Joyce. Peter, Hilary's father, was a pioneer in the organic movement with an unbounded zeal who inspired many to convert. Hilary is a chip off the old block and what she doesn't know about organic methods isn't worth knowing. Their land has been organic for 40 years and their success due to nothing but careful husbandry and hard work. The first and most important consideration is obviously the soil. Secondly, and the most variable, the weather. Their land can be soggy in season, which is good for pasture but difficult for vegetables, although brassicas are favoured. Another important thing, overlooked by many, is hedging which helps to keep soil erosion down to a minimum. Natural manures are the only permitted fertiliser, fibre levels in soil being a major consideration.

Hilary and Francis are proud of their high standards, and sometimes critical of others: the EEC standards are generally OK but allow up to 25% of an animal feedstuff to be not organically certified, which is unacceptable in their eyes. Their dairy cows have a better consistency of omega-fats because of being mostly grass fed and they claim their mince meat is more nutritious than most supermarket offerings; sometimes foodies ignore the nutritional content of a foodstuff. We talk about British buying habits. Hilary's theory, in my eyes, is that the cult of buying the cheapest thing in preference to all others is one borne out of thrift, partly a post-war mentality that is passed on by parent to offspring. Becklands gets around the price problem by selling direct, cutting out the middleman, and taking pride of place in the customer line is The White House Hotel in Charmouth, with an award-winning restaurant. They take their eggs and beef, and blackberries and even medlars, a fruit popular in medieval times.

In the seventies Peter pioneered free-range eggs. He mainly used Isa Brown and Black Rock hens although any variety of bird can be good. Isa Browns were favourites of his (Whites crossed with Rhode Island Reds). They enjoy sheltering in ditches and hedges, particularly on a hot sunny day. Temperature and light are also important as regards laying behaviour and Francis boosts the light in the coops as the days shorten towards October, to keep yield high. As demand wanes they can allow the lights to stay off for longer and leave the hens to reduce their laying frequency to a natural rate. Thus a clever farmer can harness nature to everyone's benefit – although Hilary is adamant that the public should not be over-demanding and should re-learn the benefits of seasonality. Hens are in productive life until they die, but there is nothing to beat the first 2 or 3 eggs of a hen's first laying season. They are the best. Any more advice I ask, on behalf of egg fans everywhere? Don't be obsessed by large eggs, especially jumbo eggs; and watch out – supermarket eggs can be at least 10 days old by the time they hit the shelves. Favourite egg recipes? Francis likes his eggs scrambled French-style with dandelion leaves and plenty of butter.

Chickens for eating are not much produced in Dorset but word-of-mouth led me to Mark Chilcott and his father John at Glebe Farm in Overmoigne towards Wareham. They are primarily turkey growers, particularly for Christmas, but also farm chickens, ducks and geese. Ninety per cent of their business is turkeys, White and Bronze, in four strains to take care of the size issue. They sell 10 turkeys for every goose. High standards are maintained. The birds (of all types) range freely, able to peck at anything that takes their fancy. They like stinging nettles and peck up flies, beetles and slugs although they get extra feed in the form of oats and other grains. The Chilcotts keep the fields empty for six months a year, ensuring a 'disease break' as a preventative measure, and the coops are cleaned and sterilised. They slaughter under stress-free conditions, over 20 weeks old to maximise flavour, and then the birds are hung for one week (unlike supermarkets' quick throughput methods that wet-pluck and pack immediately after slaughter). A simple philosophy for quality.

OLOROSO CHICKEN
The best-quality chicken is needed for this simple dish inspired by Andalucian cuisine.

Preheat oven to medium high (180°C/gas mark 4). Season chicken and brush with oil. Roast for 1¼-1½ hours until brown, add the raisins and pine kernels and smear the chicken with the butter, and roast for another 15 minutes. Remove from the oven, cover with foil and leave to rest for 10 minutes, which allows the flesh to release the cooking juices. Next, heat the sherry gently in a ladle over a low to medium flame and then ignite it, pouring over the bird. Joint and serve with the residue/juices poured on top. Rice would be a good accompaniment to soak up the juices.

Serves: 4
Preparation time: 5 minutes
Cooking time: 1 hour
15 minutes

1½kg free-range organic chicken (corn-fed will do)

2 tbsp olive oil

30g unsalted butter

90g raisins, soaked in brandy

90g pine kernels

1 large glass (about 75ml) dark oloroso sherry

Maldon sea salt and freshly ground black pepper

Mature lamb

JAYNE AND GEOFF Neale run their animals on a windy ridge north of Beaminster at Westleaze Farm. They specialise in lamb, wether (castrated ram), hogget (a sheep aged one to two years), mutton (over 2 year old sheep) and also have Devon Cross beef and a small show of pigs. Sheep can be eaten at around 6 months, although some breeds like Bluefaced Leicester and North Country Cheviot mature later, their eating quality improving at the 6 month to hogget stage. The Westleaze Poll Dorsets are suitable for 'young' fattening and slaughter, being good converters, (ie. good at converting grass to kilos), and lamb naturally out of season. Geoff is quite keen to experiment with cross-breeding with some of the continental breeds that fatten more easily, so they can mature without extra help in their diet. Like many other farmers I've come across, they follow organic methods, but don't seek out the Soil Association certificate. During winter the flock roams free, their diet boosted with hay, but mild winters can cause problems with pneumonia so it's not all good news.

Their most interesting success to date has been the uptake of customers willing to try mutton. Faced with a slump in the market price of lamb some years ago, they kept a small batch of 20, lucky to escape the abattoir, for 5 years and through a display at a local fete managed to tempt bold tasters to try their well-roasted meat. Prejudice about fatty 'school dinners' dissolved. Geoff had hung the meat for a good 2 weeks and people 'went mad for it!'. Now they promote it on their market banner and it pays. Certain breeds have a naturally high back fat level so they're perfect for rearing to mutton. I for one will return for the mutton sausages, slightly fatty, perfect for the chargrill, the fat melting away leaving a very tasty meaty banger. They're in the process of getting planning permission for a farm shop at Westleaze so by the time you read this, they should be in business… at home. Jayne will be ecstatic, she'll be able to show her home-made produce – like her traditional Dorset pickled eggs in cider vinegar – to best effect. Here's a suggested recipe for mutton from the Neales' kitchen

SPICY MUTTON CASSEROLE

Bone the leg of mutton (or hogget) and cut into chunks, trying not to cut them too small. Rub the meat all over with the cinnamon and nutmeg. Spread half the onion on the bottom of a casserole dish, place the meat in and then add the rest of the onion, garlic and cloves. Mix the wine with the sugar and pour it over the meat and leave to marinate for a day turning the meat from time to time. To cook, add 200ml water to the liquor, cover, and place in a slow oven (150°C/gas mark 2) for at least 2 hours or until the meat is tender.

Serves: 6
Preparation time: 24 hours
Cooking time: approx 2 hours

1 small leg of mutton
½ level tsp ground cinnamon
½ level tsp grated nutmeg
1 large onion, medium sliced
1 clove garlic, peeled
a few whole cloves
250ml robust red wine (Shiraz is good)
200g brown sugar★

★The Neales obviously have a sweeter tooth than me – I would prefer halving the sugar quantity and sautéing the onions first to sweeten them up

Suppliers

1   B V Dairy
    Wincombe Lane
    Shaftesbury
    SP7 8QD
    Tel: 01747 851855
    Web: www.bvdairy.co.uk

2   The Bakery
    Dorchester Road
    Maiden Newton
    Dorchester
    DT2 0BG
    Tel: 01300 320265

3   R J Balson & Son
    9 West Allington
    Bridport
    DT6 5BJ
    Tel: 01308 422638

4   Barrow Boar Ltd
    Foster's Farm
    South Barrow
    Yeovil
    Somerset
    BA22 7LN
    Tel: 01963 440315
    Web: www.barrowboar.co.uk

5   Becklands Farm
    Becklands Lane
    Whitchurch Canonicorum
    Bridport
    DT6 6RG
    Tel: 01297 560298
    Email: becklandsorganicfarm
    @btopenworld.com

6   Bothen Hill Produce
    7 Green Lane
    Bothenhampton
    Bridport
    DT6 4ED
    Tel: 01308 424271
    Web: www.bothenhillproduce.co.uk

7   Bride Valley Garlic Ltd.
    Outlooke Farm
    Litton Cheney
    Dorchester
    DT2 9BA
    Tel: 01308 482108

8   Bridfish Smokery
    Unit 1
    The Old Laundry Industrial Estate
    Sea Road North
    Bridport
    DT6 3BD
    Tel: 01308 456306

9   Bridget's Market
    32 East Street
    Bridport
    DT6 3LF
    Tel: 01308 427096

10 Bridport Centre For Local Food
    17 St Michael's Trading Estate
    Foundry Lane
    Bridport
    DT6 3RR
    Tel: 01308 420269
    Web: www.foodandland.org

11 The British Beekeeping Association
    National Agricultural Centre
    Stoneleigh Park
    Warwickshire
    CV8 2LG
    Tel: 02476 696679
    Web: www.bbka.org.uk

12 W J Chilcott & Co.
    Glebe Farm
    Owermoigne
    Dorchester
    DT2 8HN
    Tel: 01305 852639

13 Clipper
    Beaminster Business Park
    Broadwindsor Road
    Beaminster
    DT8 3PR
    Tel: 01308 863344
    Web: www.clipper-teas.com

14 Cranborne Chase Cheese
    The Estate Office
    Manor Farm
    Ashmore
    Nr. Salisbury
    SP5 5AE
    Tel: 01747 811125
    Email: manorfarmashmore
    @waitrose.com

15 Alan Coxon
    Coxon's Kitchen Ltd.
    PO Box 179
    Evesham
    Worcestershire
    WR11 8WN
    Web:
    www.alancoxon.com
    www.alegar.co.uk
    www.ccrs.uk.com

16 Davy's Locker
    The Old Mill
    Priory Lane
    Bridport
    DT6 3RW
    Tel: 01308 456131

17 Denhay Farms
    Broadoak
    Bridport
    DT6 5NP
    Tel: 01308 458963
    Web: www.denhay.co.uk

18 Dorset Blue Soup Company
Woodbridge Farm
Stock Gaylard
Sturminster Newton
DT10 2BD
Tel: 01963 23133
Web: www.dorsetblue.com

19 Dorset Blue Vinney
Woodbridge Farm
Stock Gaylard
Sturminster Newton
DT10 2BD
Tel: 01963 23216
Web: www.dorsetblue.com

20 The Dorset Blueberry Company
Littlemoors Farm
Ham Lane
Hampreston
Wimborne
BH21 7LX
Tel: 01202 579342
Web: www.dorset-blueberry.co.uk

21 The Dorset Brewing Co.
Brewers Quay
Hope Square
Weymouth
DT4 8TR
Tel: 01305 777515

22 Dorset Charcoal Company
Pidney
Hazelbury Bryan
Sturminster Newton
DT10 2EB
Tel: 01258 818176
Web: www.dorsetcharcoal.co.uk

23 Dorset Coppicing Limited
Sunnycorner
High Street
Spetisbury
Blandford
DT11 9DL
Tel: 01258 857225
Email: dorset.coppicingltd@virgin.net

24 Dorset Ginger Company
Bournemouth
BH9 3PL
Tel: 01202 532062

25 Dorset Pastry Ltd
Hybris Business Park
Warmwell Road
Crossways
Dorchester
DT2 8BF
Tel: 01305 854860
Web: www.dorsetpastry.com

26 Evershot Bakery
18 Fore Street
Evershot
Dorchester
DT2 0JW
Tel: 01935 83379

27 Eweleaze Farm
Osmington Hill
Osmington
DT3 6ED
Tel: 01305 833690
Web: www.eweleaze.co.uk

28 Fleet Oyster Farm & Crab House Café
Ferryman's Way
Weymouth
DT4 9YU
Tel: 01305 788867

29 Forest Products (UK) Ltd
The Old Hemp Store
North Mills
Bridport
DT6 3BE
Tel: 01308 458111
Web: www.forestproducts.co.uk

30 Fudges
Dorset Village Bakery Limited
Pinesway Business Park
Station Road
Stalbridge
DT10 2RN
Tel: 01963 362402
Web: www.fudges.co.uk

31 Henrietta Green
Food Lovers Fairs' Ltd.
Unit 203 Buspace Studios
Conlan Street
London
W10 5AP
Tel: 020 8206 6111
Web: www.foodloversbritain.com

32 Sophie Grigson
C/o DML
Claridge House
29 Barnes High Street
London
SW13 9LW
Tel: 020 8876 7560
Web: www.deborahmckenna.com

33 Hall & Woodhouse
The Brewery
Blandford St. Mary
DT11 9LS
Tel: 01258 452141
Web: www.badgerales.com

34 Valentina Harris
70 Hearnville Road
London
SW12 8RR
Tel: 020 8651 2997
Web: www.villavalentina.com

Suppliers (continued)

35 Heritage Prime @ Shedbush Farm
Muddy Ford Lane
Stanton St. Gabriel
Bridport
DT6 6DR
Tel: 01297 489304
Web: www.heritageprime.co.uk

36 Mark Hix
Caprice Holdings
28-30 Litchfield Street
London
WC2H 9NL
Tel: 020 7557 6396

37 Paul Hollywood
FA Group
40 Bowling Green Lane
Clerkenwell
London
EC1
Tel: 0700 0300 707
Web: www.paulhollywoodbreads.co.uk

38 Honeybuns
Naish Farm
Stony Lane
Holwell
Sherborne
DT9 5LJ
Tel: 01963 23597
Web: www.honeybuns.co.uk

39 The Kingcombe Centre
Toller Porcorum
Dorchester
DT2 OEQ
Tel: 01300 320684
Web: www.kingcombe-centre.demon.co.uk

40 Leakers Bakery
29 East Street
Bridport
DT6 3JX
Tel: 01308 423296

41 Long Crichel Bakery
Long Crichel
Wimborne
BH21 5JU
Tel: 01258 830852
Web: www.longcrichelbakery.co.uk

42 Long Crichel Organic Garden
Long Crichel
Wimborne
BH21 5JU
Tel: 01258 830295
Email: longcrichelgarden@cooptel.net

43 MacSorsons
Silver Street
Axminster
Devon
EX13 5AH
Tel: 01297 32253

44 Manor Farm Organic Dairy
Godmanstone
Dorchester
DT2 7AH
Tel: 01300 341415
Web: www.manor-farm-organic.co.uk

45 Meerhay Manor
Beaminster
DT8 3SB
Tel: 01308 862305
Web: www.meerhay.co.uk

46 Merchant Gourmet
2 Rollins Street
London
SE15 1EW
Tel: 0800 731 3549
Web: www.merchant-gourmet.com

47 Modbury Farm
Burton Bradstock
Bridport
DT6 4NE
Tel: 01308 897193
Web: www.modburyfarm.com

48 S Moores
Web: www.moores-biscuits.co.uk

49 Oakland's Plantation
Coldharbour
Wareham
BH20 7PA
Tel: 01929 554929

50 Ourganics Evolving Systems
Litton Lane
Litton Cheney
Dorchester
DT2 9DH
Tel: 01308 482455

51 Pampered Pigs
Rye Hill Farmhouse
Rye Hill
Bere Regis
Wareham
BH20 7LP
Tel: 01929 472327
Web: www.pampered-pigs.co.uk

52 Panary
Tel: 01722 341447
Web: www.panary.co.uk

53 Peppers By Post
Sea Spring Farm
West Bexington
Dorchester
Dorset DT2 9DD
Tel: 01308 897892
Web: www.peppersbypost.biz

54 Purbeck Ice Cream
Lower Scoles Farm
Kingston
Wareham
BH20 5LG
Tel: 01929 480090
Web: www.purbeck58icecream.co.uk

55 Purbeck Vineyard
Valley Road
Harmans Cross
Corfe Castle
BH20 5HU
Tel: 01929 481529
Web: www.purbeckvineyard.co.uk

56 River Cottage HQ
Lower Atrim Farm
Broadoak
Bridport
DT6 5PX
Web: www.rivercottage.net

57 Rural Foods
Lower Woolcombe Farm
Melbury Bubb
Dorchester
DT2 0NJ
Tel: 01935 83168
Web: www.ruralfoods.co.uk

58 Shellseekers
Ten Acres
Conygar
Broadmayne
Dorchester
DT2 8LX
Tel: 07074 104607
Email: shellseekers@talk21.com

59 N R Stoate & Sons
Cann Mills
Shaftesbury
SP7 0BL
Tel: 01747 852475
Web: www.stoatesflour.co.uk

60 The Strawberry Patch
Andy Brown
Crepe Farm Business Park
Symondsbury
Bridport
DT6 6EY
Tel: 07941 583497

61 Sunnyside Organic Farm
Lower Kingcombe
Toller Porcorum
Dorchester
DT2 0EQ
Tel: 01300 321537

62 Sydling Brook Organic Farm Shop
Up Sydling
Dorchester
DT2 9PQ
Tel: 01300 341992
Web: www.sydling.co.uk

63 Symondsbury Apple Project
The Centre for Local Food
17 St. Michael's Trading Estate
Foundry Lane
Bridport
DT6 3RR
Tel: 01308 42891
Web: www.appleproject.org.uk

64 Tamarisk Farm
West Bexington
Dorchester
DT2 9DF
Tel: 01308 897781
Web: www.tamariskfarm.com

65 The Town Mill Bakery
Mill Lane
Lyme Regis
DT7 3PU
Tel: 01297 444033
Web: www.townmill.org.uk

66 Brian J Turner CBE
Millennium Hotel
Grosvenor Square
London
W1K 2HP
Web: www.brianturneronline.co.uk

67 Washingpool Farm Shop and Restaurant
North Allington
Bridport
DT6 5HP
Tel: 01308 459549
Web: www.washingpool.co.uk

68 Lesley Waters
The Old Manor
31 Fore Street
Evershot
DT2 0JR
Tel: 01935 83700
Web: www.lesleywaters.com

69 Westleaze Farm
Whitesheet Hill
Beaminster
DT8 3SF
Tel: 01308 861408

70 Woodlands Park Dairy
Woodlands
Wimborne
BH21 8LX
Tel: 01202 822687
Web: www.woodlands-park.co.uk

71 Woolsery Cheese
The Old Dairy
Up Sydling
Dorchester
DT2 9PQ
Tel: 01300 341991
Web: www.woolserycheese.co.uk

72 Wyld Meadow Lamb
Wyld Meadow Farm
Monkton Wyld
Bridport
DT6 6DD
Tel: 01297 678318

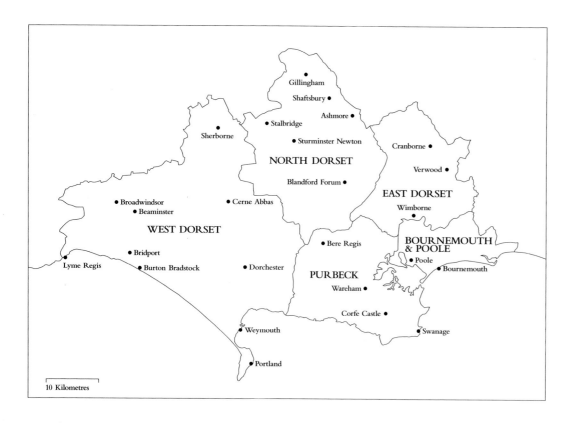

North Dorset
Ashmore: 14
Blandford Forum: 22, 23, 31, 33
Shaftesbury: 1, 59
Stalbridge: 30
Sturminster Newton: 17, 18, 19, 22

South Dorset
Corfe Castle: 54, 55
Wareham: 49, 51

East Dorset
Bournemouth: 24
Wimborne: 20, 41, 42, 70

West Dorset
Beaminster: 13, 45, 68, 69
Bridport: 3, 5, 6, 8, 9, 10, 16, 17, 29, 35, 40, 47, 56, 60, 63, 67, 72
Dorchester: 2, 7, 12, 25, 26, 39, 44, 50, 53, 57, 58, 61, 62, 64, 71
Lyme Regis: 65
Weymouth: 21, 27, 28
Sherborne: 38

Two reference points:
The Taste of The West
Agricultural House
Pynes Hill
Rydon Lane
Exeter
EX2 5ST
Tel: 01392 440745
Web: www.tasteofthewest.co.uk

Direct from Dorset
Environmental Services
County Hall
Dorchester
DT1 1XJ
Tel: 01305 224213
Web:
www.directfromdorset.org.uk

Many thanks to:
Elwell Fruit Farm
Waytown
Bridport
DT6 5LF
Tel: 01308 488283

Lytchett Heath Farm
Lytchett Matravers
Poole
BH16 6AE
Tel: 01202 621365

Conversion table (oven temperatures)

RECIPES ARE OFTEN adapted from notes specifying Aga-style instructions and I have attempted to translate these into precise settings. It should be noted, however, that all ovens differ in speed of cooking (according to internal design, arrangement and size) so use your common sense when reaching for consistent results and pay attention to the level/height of shelf employed in the baking process. Turn joints and trays around during cooking if it is a fan-assisted oven; and it is generally advisable to turn the dial down by 10° in this case, to mimic a traditional thermo-convecting oven. Do not overcrowd the oven and ensure hot air has space to circulate evenly around the items being cooked.

Gas mark	Fahrenheit	Celsius
1	275	140
2	300	150
3	325	170
4	350	180
5	375	190
6	400	200
7	425	220
8	450	230
9	475	240

Index

Recipes

Foodstuffs, and where to find them
(A list of the sources as mentioned in this book, but of course there are many more around the county.)

Thanks

A book for charity of this scale and scope, necessarily a year-long project, being completed in spare time, is an immense undertaking. It would not have been possible for me to complete the task without the support and goodwill of the following:

Claire Whitehead, the driving force behind the initiative – who brought the team together, saw it through from inception to distribution, and managed (sometimes) to get me to write text on cold winter mornings.

Brian Neesam, for a keen eye on the images, producing a range of photographs of the county second to none, and his wife Juli, for helping with research, the minutiae of photographic administration, keeping Brian on track, and great strong coffee.

Mike Bone, the designer at Bostock and Pollitt, needs a big mention for putting up with all our chopping and changing and lending his expertise to turn a small local idea into a book that will have big impact on the eye and in time, we trust, on the charities' reserves. Thanks must also be extended to Nick Pollitt for enabling Mike to commit to this year-long project – his generosity is greatly appreciated.

Emma Treichl, publisher, for having the foresight in the first place, the confidence in getting me on board and commitment to kick-start this project.

Michael Treichl for his support, and the Parnham House staff for their help, especially Hayley of the garden staff.

Helen Carless, the charity's representative, for guidance and support, and the committee of workers who gave of their time and energy: Rose Joly, Sophie Digby, Tilly McMaster, Annette Smallwood, Diana Pinney and Tessa Russell.

Special thanks must be given to Antonia Johnson, who had the unenviable task of editing the text under very tight deadlines and to whom I am grateful for keeping the flavour of the book intact.

Bridget Swann deserves thanks for permission to abridge extracts of my text published in *Dorset* magazine from my 'Nosh' food column.

Michael and Joy Michaud deserve a shout for helpful advice for this book and for unsung heroic work to put Bridport on the map as the centre of food excellence in the south west.

John & Gill Tester for kind loan of kitchen facilities and impromptu styling.

Finally, I would like to extend my personal gratitude to all the producers mentioned in Eat Dorset for their vital goodwill. Many local people gave of their time and effort to show the fine produce of this county in its best light; their energies spent improving our land will be a fitting legacy for our children and a source of inspiration to others for generations. They should be proud.

Mike Feasey

Brian would like to thank the following people who know what they have done to help:

Nichola Motley; Geof and Ann Parker; John and Gill Tester; Angela, Malcolm, Rachel and James at Millers Farm Shop, Axminster; Nigella Lawson; Linda Hooper at The Blue Anchor Café, West Bexington; Philip and Connie at Shatcombe Farm; Tina at MacSorsons Fishmonger, Axminster; Harry May of the Marie F, Lyme Regis.

Special thanks to Dave Walsh, Sharon Johnston and Paul Collins at Bostock and Pollitt for retouching and production of the book.

Finally, Jacob, Dexter, Mary and Curtis for missing out on a summer holiday.

Brian Neesam

Mike Feasey (left) has a long food history: a chef in the 80s, a London restaurateur in the 90s (The Nosh Brothers); a writer of 4 books including *Entertaining with The Nosh Brothers* and *Indulgence* (Macmillan), he has also written and presented several television series on food and travel for Carlton Food Network. He currently writes a monthly food and drink column for *Dorset* magazine and works as a food consultant, taking on jobs large (film location catering) and small (local dinner parties).

Brian Neesam lives just over the border in East Devon, but holds the Dorset larder close to his heart, and stomach! His experience spans 20 years, photographing many an advertising campaign (for British Telecom, British Airways and The Greater London Authority to name but a few). Since moving to Devon, his love of the countryside has spilled over into his work and he is now compiling a library of photographs of landscapes and farming.